Outstanding School Leadership

Other titles from Bloomsbury Education

A Manifesto for Excellence in Schools by Rob Carpenter
Lighting the Way by Angela Browne
Riding the Waves by James Hilton
Stepping into Senior Leadership by Jon Tait
The Authentic Leader by Andrew Morrish
The Headteacher's Handbook by Rae Snape

Outstanding School Leadership

How to take your school to the top and stay there

Peter J Hughes

BLOOMSBURY EDUCATION

LONDON OXFORD NEW YORK NEW DELHI SYDNEY

BLOOMSBURY EDUCATION
Bloomsbury Publishing Plc
50 Bedford Square, London, WC1B 3DP, UK
29 Earlsfort Terrace, Dublin 2, Ireland

BLOOMSBURY, BLOOMSBURY EDUCATION and the Diana logo are trademarks of
Bloomsbury Publishing Plc

First published in the UK, 2023 by Bloomsbury Publishing Plc

Text copyright © Peter J Hughes, 2023

'Windy day' illustration copyright p. 76 © designed by Storyset - Freepik.com, 2023

'Elephant' illustration copyright pp. xvii, 12, 77, 100 © Flaticon.com, 2023

Author biography photo copyright © Lucienne Jacobs, 2023

All other illustrations copyright © Peter J Hughes, 2023

All contributions are copyright of the contributor named.

Peter Hughes has asserted his right under the Copyright, Designs and Patents Act,
1988, to be identified as Author of this work

Bloomsbury Publishing Plc does not have any control over, or responsibility for, any
third-party websites referred to or in this book. All internet addresses given in this
book were correct at the time of going to press. The author and publisher regret any
inconvenience caused if addresses have changed or sites have ceased to exist, but can
accept no responsibility for any such changes

All rights reserved. No part of this publication may be reproduced or transmitted in
any form or by any means, electronic or mechanical, including photocopying,
recording, or any information storage or retrieval system, without prior
permission in writing from the publishers

A catalogue record for this book is available from the British Library

ISBN: PB: 978-1-8019-9329-6; ePDF: 978-1-8019-9328-9; ePub: 978-1-8019-9331-9

2 4 6 8 10 9 7 5 3 1 (paperback)

Typeset by Newgen KnowledgeWorks Pvt. Ltd., Chennai, India
Printed and bound in the UK by CPI Group Ltd, CR0 4YY

To find out more about our authors and books visit www.bloomsbury.com
and sign up for our newsletters

Acknowledgements

I want to thank my family in Australia, and my London family – I love you all.

To my teaching colleagues and support staff, your time, passion, patience and support have been invaluable.

A special thank you to the late Veronica Carol, Rob Walker and Ray Fergeson. I now know how truly lucky I was to have worked with these selfless leaders. I was blessed to know them and be led by them.

To those who have supported me throughout the process of writing this book, especially those who attended the table reading; your feedback was invaluable. A heartfelt thank you to Patricia, who both contributed to the table reading and has selflessly created the maps within this book.

I am also very grateful to the amazing leaders who have shared their stories so freely. To my partner Danielle, who has both contributed to this book and spent many hours diligently capturing all my thoughts and ideas. Thank you for believing in me, being proud of me and loving me every day.

Lastly, I am particularly grateful to all the children I have had the pleasure of teaching over the years or who have attended one of our schools. This dedication is for you, as you are the true inspiration for this book.

Contents

Foreword by Matthew Jones OBE ix

Preface xiii

Anti-racism *co-authored by Danielle Lewis-Egonu* xix

1. **Background: Who am I?** 1

2. **Being mission-driven** 17

3. **Doing what is right, not what is popular** 39

4. **Taking risks** 63

5. **A relentless focus on finding and developing talent** 81

6. **Teaching and learning above all** 103

7. **Relationships** 121

8. **Big shoes to fill** 143

9. **Where to from here?** 159

Further reading 161

References 163

Index 167

Author Biography 170

Foreword

By Matthew Jones OBE

Executive Chair and Founder, Elephant Group; Executive Principal, Ark Globe and Evelyn Grace Academy

I first realised the significance of attending an excellent school when, at the age of 11, my mother decided not to send me to the nearest secondary school. Instead, she chose a school that was two bus rides and almost four miles away from the council estate in West London where we lived.

My mother's decision raised all sorts of questions for an 11-year-old, who just wanted to attend the same school as his friends. Why did I have to make a 40-minute bus journey to school? What's wrong with my local school? What is so good about the other school? To this day, I cannot thank my mother enough for ignoring my tantrums at the time and for sending me halfway across West London to ensure that I received a quality education. It was transformational.

At their best, schools can alter the trajectory of a young person's life through strong academics, instilling values and developing character. They can introduce students to new 'worlds', both real and imagined, inspire ambition and self-confidence, and expose them to networks and opportunities beyond their usual spheres of influence.

If, as a nation, we are to maximise the latent talent throughout our country, we need to establish excellent schools in every community so that all children can pursue their passions and develop the skills required for their chosen careers. However, access to a 'great' school continues to be elusive for too many families and children, especially for those families at the lower end of the income bracket. The inequality in education provision between the 'haves' and 'have nots' remains one of the most significant injustices faced by disadvantaged families up and down the county. That is why any book that attempts to codify the process of creating excellent schools, and how to sustain them, is worth its weight in gold, especially if its author is someone who has the rare distinction of leading one of the most successful schools and MATs in England.

I have known Peter for well over a decade. My first encounter with Peter was back in 2009, when he was vice-principal at Mossbourne Community Academy and presented their approach to tracking student achievement to a group of aspiring headteachers. As anyone who knew Peter at that time would expect, the session was delivered with his usual assurance and precision. However, the aspect of the presentation that struck me most was his optimism and uncompromising belief that all children, regardless of their background, can achieve well, given the right support and consistent high-quality teaching. Today, this may seem like an uncontroversial notion, thanks to the success of schools like Mossbourne Community Academy but back then, few leaders in education were bold enough to say it out loud.

Over the years I have got to know Peter extremely well, due to our engagement in the 'Future Leaders' programme and through our mutual friend and fellow Future Leader Glen Denham. Whether we were attending a leadership event or catching up socially, our conversations were almost exclusively focused on teaching and learning, student achievement and how we can be better leaders. It came as no surprise to me that when Peter took over the daunting task of leading Mossbourne Community Academy after Sir Michael Wilshaw's departure, the school continued to be a beacon of educational excellence. This was by no means inevitable. After the departure of a successful and high-profile leader, many schools serving disadvantaged communities experience a period of decline. The fact that Mossbourne Community Academy continued to thrive is testament to Peter's drive, resilience and systematic approach to school leadership.

In this book, Peter shares details of his upbringing and the experiences that have shaped him as a person and as a leader. Through anecdotes, case studies and some education and business theory, Peter explains his approach to creating sustainable schools that provide a safe environment for young people to thrive. He shares his views on the leadership characteristics and competencies needed to lead schools in challenging contexts. The book explains the key 'ingredients' needed and provides practical examples of how strategic decisions are made and how to implement plans with fidelity. Peter also reveals some of the mistakes that he has made and the lessons learned in the hope that others don't make similar errors. I found 'Umbrella-gate' particularly enlightening.

Reading this book will be of interest to anyone committed to state education. There is something in it for policymakers, those hoping to lead their own school, existing headteachers and multi-academy trust (MAT) CEOs (chief executive officers). The fact that Peter is still rooted to the community of his schools, which he has served for well over a decade, gives the book a level of authenticity and relevance that is not often present in publications about education leadership. To this day, Peter continues to be ambitious for his schools and for the families and children of Hackney. It is my hope that readers of this book will be inspired by Peter's sense of mission and relentless focus on school improvement, so that they too will take up the mantle of building high-performing schools in communities that need them.

There is no greater privilege than creating an awesome school that inspires and empowers young people, especially those currently underserved by the education system. Yet there is still no greater challenge.

Preface

I have worked in education for over 25 years – ¼ of a century, 5^2, $\sqrt{625}$ (sorry, my maths brain sometimes just spits out random facts; I'll get back to the story) – a decade of which I have been a principal, executive principal and, eventually, a MAT CEO in the London Borough of Hackney.

But my life didn't start here. I'm an immigrant. I arrived in the United Kingdom in 2001, when I was 25 years old, the same age that my older brother was when he died. I was born in Sydney, Australia, the middle of three children. Throughout this book you will learn about my leadership journey, be provided with insights and practical tools that you can use for your journey and learn about my life and my upbringing, which was a turbulent one. There are whispers of the impact of these experiences interwoven throughout my leadership practice, knowledge and skills displayed within the chapters.

I tell you this not only as a trigger warning, as some may find the stories of my past a challenge to read, but also to give you an insight into why this leadership book is structured very differently to most. My story is unique, but I do not want you, the reader, to think that you cannot attain the achievements that I have accomplished or soar to even greater heights because your story is different to mine. Quite the contrary – I want you to find the leader within yourself. I offer you the benefit of knowing my story in the hope that it can help you, in some small way, on your way to great things.

Striving for and maintaining exceptional leadership is a challenge, but it is a worthwhile and achievable one. This book seeks to offer you a blueprint and framework to use and build upon with your own style and flare because, after all, are we not all unique with something rare and wonderful to offer? Another thing that you may have already noticed is that I will talk to you, the reader, a lot. I'm breaking the fourth wall intentionally in order to model a scenario of us having a chat over a flat white, around a campfire or in a mentoring session.

We all take different paths to leadership, and we all have different leadership styles that reflect our personalities, backgrounds and beliefs, both professional and personal. Although books on leadership will attempt to put us into a box or to simplify the complexity of it by reducing it into a 2x2 grid, it is my belief that we learn as much about leadership from watching and listening to expert practitioners as we do from reading the theory. Over the decades, I have built up a series of observations upon which I can draw, where I have seen amazing leaders deal with a range of issues. I also have a bank of detailed stories shared with me about how people have dealt with all manner of situations. Some of this wisdom I've collected over the years has come from mentors, some of it from friends and some of these gifts have been given to me from people outside of education. Over nearly three decades, I have also developed my own knowledge of education and business theory that I can draw upon as situations arise.

When thinking about this book, I wanted to ensure that it was easier to navigate than some other books with which I've attempted to engage myself, so that the reader can dip in and out of it and focus on the chapters how they please. The other reason why this was an important element for me is because I've always struggled to read. Many professionals have said that I'm dyslexic but I've never been tested. What I do know is that I read at a speed of less than a third of that of most of my senior leadership team (SLT), and over the years I have naturally made adaptations to the world around me that have still allowed me to achieve many of my goals – one of which was completing an Executive MBA from Oxford University. It was a wonderful experience and achievement for me, a working-class country boy from Oz. One from which my schools and I gained hugely in many ways over the years. It was also the catalyst for turning the teaching improvement software platform ProgressTeaching©, which I developed for the Mossbourne schools, into a business. My life outside of the school setting offers a rich insight into leadership and, as a result, there will be references to my upbringing and to business theory and practice throughout this book.

Let's talk about the book's structure

Each chapter focuses on one of eight elements that have been instrumental in my own career and are, in my opinion, essential to creating great schools. The chapters are structured in a way that should give rise to discussion, engage your 'thinking outside the box' skills, present frameworks from which to work and give examples of leadership experiences from across the world, roles and sectors.

The chapter structure consists of:

Introduction: A brief summary of the topic being explored in the chapter.
The yarn: This is the Australian word for a story. For me, when I think of a yarn, I visualise two people leaning over a fencepost, standing around

their ute (utility vehicle) or sitting by the campfire swapping stories about their experience from that day or from some point in the past. The beauty of a yarn is that you are not always sure where it is going to go, but it will reveal itself in the end. When you live in the outback, you have time, and therefore time has a different quality about it. Yarns pass on knowledge but also entertain. For this reason, they meander and appear at times to drift off topic. I want you as the reader to enjoy the yarns. We do promote reading for pleasure after all.

Leadership skills: I acknowledge that each chapter may be a platform for debate. Therefore, I have incorporated research and further reading where relevant. These additions seek to help frame subsequent conversations that rely on research evidence to have a solid foundation. Each chapter unpicks some of the leadership skills listed below, to offer further insight, information and a holistic view. I focus on these skills because they are often overlooked, and each chapter only looks at the skill/s relevant to the chapter topic. For clarity, skills like communication, active listening, goal-setting and the like are important for leaders, and there are many books, websites and TED Talks that will tell you about them and their importance.

Analysis: Detailed examination of anything in order to understand it.

Background: The circumstances or situation prevailing at a particular time or underlying a particular event.

Exploration: The action of exploring an unfamiliar area.

Research: The collecting of information about a particular subject.

Scrutiny: Critical observation or examination.

Case study: These are stories combined with actionable insights from leaders with experience of the topic discussed in the chapter. They offer you an opportunity to see patterns and causes of leadership behaviours. They include insights from people I know with a range of leadership experiences.

The solution: An answer. Something that you can take away and use in your own environment straight away if needed.

The final words: This section provides a conclusion on the contents of the chapter and offers you my own reflections on the topic as a whole.

Top tips: Quite simply, these are pointers that will fit on a sticky note that can be kept in a notebook, diary or laptop screen as a quick reference point and reminder for later.

From the structure, you can see that the book will be part autobiographical, part yarn (story) and part theory. The aim of this book is to help you, the aspiring leader or the leader already in post, to improve your leadership practice. But if you have arrived here out of curiosity because you are someone interested in education or learning more about me and my journey, then I hope you enjoy the story. I know what it's like to be the first one in school before 7.00 am and the last to leave after 7.00 pm, while still questioning whether or not you've done enough that day. The advice I provide is intended to be both practical and thought-provoking. I know that my drive home is often my time to decompress and let my mind ponder on a key question or scenario, so I hope that this book gives you a few questions at a time to consider, as you read through the chapters. This book deals with huge themes relating to school leadership, while recognising that incremental shifts are required to bring about lasting change and longevity. Building exceptional schools is like running a neverending marathon and not a sprint; you need a steady pace to survive.

Last few things from me

I make no apology for telling stories about my experience, as I feel that these anecdotes provide insights that might just help the reader to pinpoint the problems in front of them and see the solution more clearly. Being a leader in education is not easy, and my aim is that this book will give you the knowledge to develop the skills that you need, both known and unknown.

Phrases and terms

For clarity and to avoid confusion, I want to highlight the terminology that is used throughout this book in order for us to have a common understanding.

- I use the term 'principal' throughout the book, but it also encompasses CEO, headteacher, head of school, etc.
- When I use the word 'school', I want you to think about your own organisation, whether that be a MAT, a primary school, a PRU (pupil referral unit), a specialist setting, an EYFS (Early Years Foundation Stage) centre, etc. I've used this word as a universal term. I didn't want to use the word 'organisation' repeatedly, as it just doesn't fit the school context.

- I have often used the names of my sisters and brothers when creating amalgamated characters – for example, Dallas (my brother) is the name of the Good King. Some people's names have been altered to protect their identity. In their places, I've used the names of other family members and close friends as an homage.

- Throughout this book, I will say 'my trust', 'my school' and 'my children' because, for me, it is my trust and my school and they are my children. I highlight this because the success of the federation is not mine alone, and some may mistakenly believe that my use of language implies that I think it is. Although these words imply ownership, I don't own Mossbourne, just like a parent doesn't own a child; I am but its custodian. Therefore, I will use the words 'I', 'we' and 'our' interchangeably.

And last but not least, look out for the elephants.

Anti-racism

The section is co-authored by Danielle Lewis-Egonu.

Everything about this section of the book is deliberate. It is placed right after the introduction and before Chapter 1 (Who am I?) because I can't talk about myself or anything to do with leadership until we discuss race. It is titled 'Anti-racism' because it is not enough to say that I'm not a racist, for if we are simply non-racist, then we are tacitly agreeing to racism. It is co-authored with my partner Danielle Lewis-Egonu because, although I can champion anti-racism, it is only by listening to people who have lived the experience that one can hope to deepen their understanding of the challenges that people of colour face every day – the challenges created by other people and the fundamental structures of society.

For the White readers, especially those in positions of power, I want to remind you that it is our responsibility to be allies, to champion anti-racism and to speak up – to bring the race conversation into the spaces where it needs to be. This isn't White guilt and isn't about lowering standards. It is about challenging that status quo and asking the question 'Is this equity?' If the system is stacked against someone, then it is everyone's job to do something about it.

It is easy to say, 'What about the White working class? Don't we need to ensure that they get a fair chance?' They, the White working class as a group, have some of the weakest outcomes in the country and the lowest progression rate to university. To that, I say yes, we do need to do more for our White working-class (free-school-meals) children, especially the boys. They are *my* people after all. For me, it is not an either/or scenario. There are those that delight at pitching the White working class against people of colour, but we know that the working class in England is no longer just White, but a mixture of people from all ethnic backgrounds. The reality is, that as educators, it is our role to create a fairer society for all.

This chapter has an especially important role for me as a leader in Hackney – a leader of a multicultural MAT that serves a pupil population that is 65 per cent people of colour. For me, the anti-racist journey is a perpetual one; it's not going to be over once we find the 'magic policy'. It is a journey, I am sad to say, that I feel will be with us for the rest of my life.

As an organisation, we have:

- placed anti-racism as an agenda item on every board meeting until we feel that it is resolved; all my principals and I must answer to our progress in this area at every meeting
- provided racial literacy training to all members of the Mossbourne Family
- started work on the race equality mark
- implemented the Rooney Rule (part of the NFL's effort to develop a deep, sustainable talent pool at all levels of the organisation: https://operations. nfl.com/inside-football-ops/inclusion/the-rooney-rule) for all SLT posts and above
- implemented a programme to accelerate teachers of colour into middle and senior leadership positions
- set ourselves a target to have our teaching body and leadership teams reflect the community that they serve.

But there are other things that we can share and do using our own lived experience. For example, I take every opportunity to share with my pupils that I am an immigrant. I want them to know that immigrants come in all colours, and that the news is biased and pushing a vision of immigrants as 'the non-White unwelcome kind that are taking over the country'.

Danielle

I agree with and support what Peter says here in this chapter, and although daunting, because I am ever-aware of the power of words and their magnitude, I feel privileged to have the opportunity to contribute my part to this co-authored section and, ultimately, to this book.

Neither of us are setting ourselves up to be the examples for the world to use, and I say this as a woman of colour, who has reached a position in education that many haven't and still face significant barriers to achieve. I am aware that I am an outlier. I buck the trend of expectations and statistics. The higher roles in education are incredibly hard places to get to, and once there, it can be a lonely place to be without allies. I am fortunate to have encountered allies along the way, who have been monumental in my life. I wear many labels, which the world has bestowed upon me, and which have often also been used to pass judgement. But, much like Peter, the richness of my life, and the experiences that I've had, have given me an insight into the world that has deepened my understanding of the people I have served and continue to serve throughout my life and career.

It may sound strange, but I didn't realise I was something other than the 'norm' until the world gave me a label in an attempt to try to define me in the way it wished. As I was growing up, words used to hurt people who looked like me became more frequent and overt. I'd always been aware of the staring and the whispers as a child, especially when I called out for my mum in the park. People would look at us, my mother and me – a White woman picking up her Brown child – and often whisper and point as she answered my call. I was also regularly told by my peers in primary that my mum couldn't be my mum because we didn't look the same, which would often lead me to question my being and what I knew to be true about myself. I tell you this because my earliest memories demonstrate that my skin colour invited people to question and judge me without invitation and without regard to the fact that I was a child, who would be damaged by this. I never felt like I belonged because I was something other than the 'norm'.

My father was an immigrant, coming to England as part of the Windrush generation, bringing with him the legacy of carnival from his homeland of Trinidad, as well as the name of the owners who enslaved my ancestors. My mother, borne of a settled Irish traveller, gave me the love of Irish stew and dumplings, as well as the secrets to guard of our traveller background and family. Neither had raised a half-breed, half-caste, half-child before in a world that liked to label things and put them in boxes, and therefore they couldn't equip me with the skills to face the world that I encountered. I've seen and felt many changes in our society throughout my lifetime, but yes, there are still times when I am made to feel that I don't belong.

I do not underestimate the impact of the position that I am in and the remarkable people around me, including Peter, who have something to offer us all. Each of us are remarkable creatures who have something to give the world, to the people we care about and to the communities that we serve. It is our responsibility to make that manifest. We inherit everything that defines us as individuals, both internally and externally. The combination of our genetic make-up and our interactions with our environments and others makes us unique but also forever unfinished. And isn't that a beautiful thing? We forever have the capacity to grow, evolve and learn from the people that we encounter. This is why it is important that we talk around the proverbial campfires and break bread with each other.

It is little steps that get us to the end goals – the relentless decision to continue even when it's hard. Even when it's uncomfortable. Even when there is disbelief. My very existence embodies and is evidence of the institutional racism within my country – the country in which I was born and raised and which I love. This is a hard truth, but it is an essential one to hear because there is no one to fight, as I would be fighting myself. Instead, we must learn together and find a way forward, to ensure that children don't enter our world feeling like they don't belong in their own home.

So, where to from here?

For us, it is about the conversation. It is about the children. We believe that the only way forward is to discuss race and class in an open way where people don't feel silly, put down or marginalised. When the 'PC police' or 'the cancellers' get involved, the problem doesn't get solved; it goes underground, only to resurface, darker and more sinister than before. Debating an opposing view that you can see and hear is easy; fighting one that is hidden underground is impossible.

We are reminded of the movie *The Best of Enemies*, based on a true story, where the town had a charrette, to agree where the black children would be educated, following a fire in the 'coloured' school. If a Ku Klux Klan leader and a civil rights activist can become lifelong friends, then surely anything is possible.

We want to leave you with a question. How do we create a world where all the children we serve feel like they belong?

1 Background: Who am I?

School (not education) has always held an important place in my heart, but not for the reasons you may initially think. Like most people working in education, it has been a constant in my life from the age of four. However, my appreciation for school stands out for me in particular, due to my fragmented early life caused by my turbulent upbringing. Throughout the first 15 years of my life, there were periods of relative stability punctuated with periods of instability, where it felt like moving was the only constant. The age of 15 is poignant for me, as it was when I found my new home with an adopted family and officially became what is now known as a looked-after child (LAC).

I use this chapter to give you an insight into the person that I was and am today. This isn't a requirement by any means, but I do feel that this insight will give you, the reader, if you so wish, a deeper understanding of my motivations and decisions and the challenges that I have encountered. I do not wish to use this chapter to insinuate that these lived experiences have made me a better leader than someone without them, but they have given me a knowledge bank and perspective that are unique for someone in my position, and it is for this reason that I offer you the opportunity to learn a little bit about me here. I will also share an ode to Hackney and introduce you to Dipo Odunsi, my Chief Operations Officer (COO), who will share some of his experiences and thoughts about my leadership. This chapters ends with a few reflections.

My Yarn

So, I will start at the very beginning. I was born in Sydney, the capital city of New South Wales, Australia.

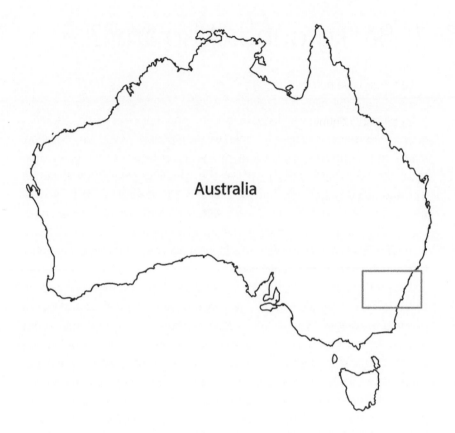

Australia

My mother and father had many challenges; neither had the capacity to nurture and care for children in the way that you would expect in a family home, and both of them had very limited education. For my mum, this meant that she was and still is illiterate. I am positioned as the middle child of my mum's three children and the eldest child from my parents' on and off relationship. My older brother shouldered a lot of the responsibility of caring for my sister and me, as well as trying to keep us safe, not only due to my parents' fragmented relationship but also due to the shortfalls of our mother, who never received the help that she needed to overcome her own generational battles. In today's terms, he would be considered a young carer, but to me he was my big brother and I adored him.

I always had chores. In one of the first homes that I remember living in, we needed to chop wood to fuel the stove. Without a lit stove, there was no hot water and no ability to cook. For this reason, long before I finished primary school, I was proficient at chopping firewood. I don't look at chopping wood out of necessity as a bad thing; all children had chores, and chopping wood was mine. It means that I have many fond memories of the smell and taste of toast being cooked by my brother on the open fire. I also have fond memories of primary school from my childhood.

I attended five primary schools across my home state of New South Wales, due mainly to the nature of my parents' relationship. I spent longer at some (five years, not continuous) than others (two weeks), but each school marks key moments and memories within my life. Cootamundra, Binalong, Mt Pritchard, Liverpool, John Warby and even a few stints at the Royal Far West (www.royal farwest.org.au), a hospital-based school, all gave me the opportunity to see my strengths as a young pup.

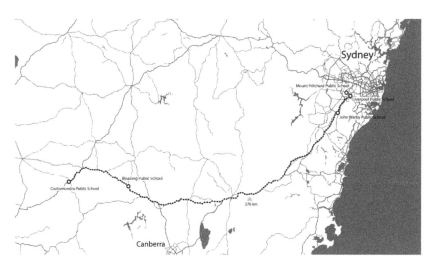

At school I felt safe. I remember loving to run at breaktimes, and I have fond memories of times tables competitions. At one of my schools, we had roller skating sessions for sport because the great thing about the New South Wales education system is that all schools do sport on a Wednesday afternoon, every week. I remember being good at maths. I enjoyed singing on a Thursday afternoon, when we sang along with the radio broadcast in the classroom. Although I still can't sing, it has never stopped me from trying. However, I have distinct memories of struggling with writing and reading, getting things wrong and not being able to pronounce my spelling words. The only time I got all my spellings correct was when I learned them in order and the teacher tested us in that exact same order. Despite this, I had an overriding sensation that school was a nice place to be. I always felt that the teachers were caring and attentive.

It was at the age of seven when I was involved in a chainsaw accident. This horrific incident happened while my mum was cutting wood with the chainsaw and we (my siblings and I) were collecting it from the ground and loading it into the trailer. For me, this resulted in hospital stays and surgery on my arm to repair it. Once my arm was better, I was determined to learn how to swim. Due to the accident (and subsequent hospital stays), I'd missed this opportunity and was upset because my little sister could swim and I couldn't. I distinctly remember wanting to go in the deep end of the local pool, but knowing that I had to be able to swim a length before I would be allowed to. I enlisted the help of my peers; they told and showed me the basics and off I went practising until I was able to pass the pool owner's test to swim a length in order to access the deep end with my friends.

My primary years were unstructured and full of adverse childhood experiences, but they were also the years that developed my resilience and problem-solving skills, as well as an appreciation of the need for reciprocity in life. At the end of primary school, I could read and write but I would, in today's environment, probably have been identified as being a child who was dyslexic. I use a great deal of mental energy to read and write. I've had lots of practice, of course, at developing these skills, so have picked up some useful hacks and aids along the way to help me with reducing the cognitive load. I still read more slowly than the members on my senior leadership team and writing still takes focus and effort, but I have still been able to accomplish many personal goals.

It wasn't until my early teens that I realised my mum couldn't read, and it wasn't until I was much older, when I became a teacher, that I started to connect the dots of my experiences in school and the difficulty that I had with reading and writing. As most children do throughout primary school, I would bring books home from school, sit down excitedly and try to read my book. If I got stuck on a word, I would seek support from my mum, asking her to read it to me. I recall her telling me words as I listened intently. It wasn't until I was much older (and I can't pinpoint exactly when or where) that I realised she had been making up the words, as she had no ability to read them herself. Instead of being honest with me, with herself and with the world, she very successfully masked to her young son her inability to decode the words on the pages in front of her. This epiphany helped me to understand my own challenges – to acknowledge them but also to realise that they are not an excuse. I've had to work harder than most due to my difficulties with words, but I am thankful that it has not stopped me from moving forwards.

Although I often fell behind in some subjects in primary school, it was clear very early on that I had an aptitude for mathematics. There was something special about how I just 'got' and understood maths as a child. I enjoyed my interactions with it and the lessons, no matter what school I attended at the time. It's hard for me to articulate why I have such a skill in this area. The best way that I feel I can describe it is that as the maths got harder, it made more sense to me because my mind was hard-wired for problem-solving.

As an individual, I understand the struggles that many children in my own primary schools face with reading difficulties, disruptive home environments and a lack of a sense of belonging. As a mathematician and someone who in their early career often dismissed literacy as not being my responsibility, I have come to realise that I couldn't have been more wrong.

As time progressed, my parents finally stopped the on-again and off-again saga of their relationship and parted ways for good. This didn't, however, stop my disruptive home life. As I entered the secondary school phase of my life, the fragmented schooling continued. I floated across the state, attending three further schools: Airds High School, Quandialla Central School and Young Technology High School. The impact of this continuously splintered education was, in simple terms, huge. I was in a never-ending cycle of playing catch-up, while still carrying the weight of the ongoing anguish from my homelife. As a child now growing into a young man, I had to develop further resilience to adjust to both internal and external demands through necessity.

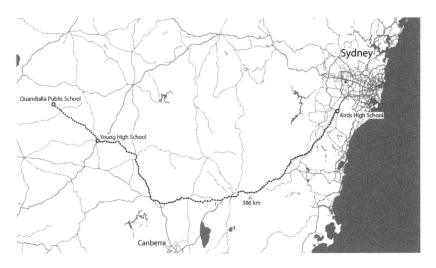

My adaptability helped me to learn to navigate the school system and to survive the constant changes and challenges with which I was faced. This meant that I wasn't always the best-behaved boy at school, although I wouldn't have ever called myself a naughty child. Now in secondary, the challenges that I faced going into new settings was different. I was having to adjust to accepting a new label of 'teenager' and tackling the ripple effect that I made (both positive and negative) when arriving as the new boy in each high school. Despite these varied and sometimes negative experiences, I always felt comfortable within the space of a classroom during lessons in school. I did, however, struggle with the social dynamics that came with peer groups and daily school life as I entered this phase of life, which I'm sure many reading this can relate to.

As stated at the beginning of this chapter, it was at this point in my life that I found a family who would give me the security and stability that I needed, until this day. At 13 years old, my dad and stepmum split. This meant that my sister and I needed to leave and find somewhere else to live. I couldn't stay with my dad and it wasn't possible to stay with my mum either. My sister and I were torn from each other, as the only options available to us were to be placed separately with family friends hundreds of miles apart in Yass and Quandialla respectively. It was in Quandialla that I met Dallas, who would become my adopted brother, and my life would take a new and unexpected path.

It's incredible for me to reflect back on my journey through education in my early years of life and detail the elements that contributed to where I am now. This journey has significantly influenced my viewpoint and my decision-making around many aspects of my career and life. It's given me the gift of a unique perspective for someone in a role like mine. The country boy from Oz moving from school to school, navigating a challenging childhood, could never have imagined becoming a CEO of a MAT in the heart of London, England, with an office overlooking Hackney Downs Park, East London.

But my yarn doesn't stop at high school. Life has a strange serendipity to it. In the Australian educational system, and especially in my final school, Young Technology High School, it was normal for almost everyone to continue onto Years 11 and 12 (known as sixth form in England). The only people who didn't had an apprenticeship to be a plumber, sparky, chippy, etc. This made it a non-choice and I found myself in a position where I was able to continue my studies with the possibility of going to university. In Australia, the name of the qualification that you obtain varies from state to state; every state is awarded a 'Certificate of Education', with the exception of my home state, New South Wales, who awards a Higher School Certificate.

At the end of Year 12 (back in 1992), students received a score known as the Tertiary Entrance Rank (TER), which would allow them entry into universities. Why is this important? Well, against all odds, I sat my end-of-year exams and received a TER rank high enough to propel me to the next leg of my journey, which was to study a Bachelor of Education (secondary mathematics) at Charles Sturt University. If my adopted family hadn't taken me in and moved to Young, I would not have had the opportunity of the 'non-choice' at Young Technology

High School. This automatic expectation to attend sixth form, and university as a result, would not even have been a thought for me.

I didn't want to go to university; I wanted to join the Air Force, and I definitely never wanted to be a teacher. So I can thank my friend Raj for this part of my journey. Raj completed a university application for me as a joke. He wanted to be a teacher and still is back home but, I reiterate, I did not. I realised that his joke had become reality when I saw my name in the *Sydney Morning Herald* (an Australian newspaper, a bit like *The Times*) where they printed all of the students' names who had been accepted to universities. This annual printing of young pups' names was a big event, but it wasn't even me who saw it at first; it was everyone else in town who spotted it and proceeded to tell me that my name was there – my name, **Peter John Hughes**, as bold as this. I would be studying a four-year Bachelor of Education (secondary mathematics) at Charles Sturt University. This would become the first step in my journey to becoming the CEO of a MAT in Hackney.

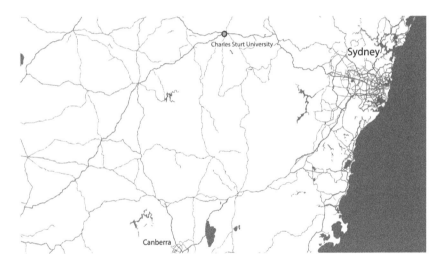

A salute to Hackney

As an Australian, I have an affinity with the strong sense of identity and belonging in Hackney. It mirrors how we Australians feel about our home. People are proud of being from, living in and working in Hackney, and that also includes me. I love the juxtaposition and diversity that the borough contains; it speaks to me on so many levels of my being, the reasons of which I'm sure you can see now you have read a small snapshot of my life. Where else do you have all the different diasporas, cultures and economic backgrounds living together, going to the same school and being appreciated for their differences? Hackney is such a unique place that you can't help but fall in love with it.

But Hackney has not always felt so fondly of me.

> *'It's critical: Seek first to understand, then to be understood. Seeking real understanding affirms the other person and what they have to say. That's what they want.' (Stephen Covey, 1989, p. 196)*

On more than one occasion, people have shared with me the stories and perceptions of me and my institution. There has been a perception that I am cold-hearted and don't care about children and that the institution I run is an inhumane Stalinist bootcamp. I have been misunderstood by many, and did not prioritise the time to dispel any myths formed about me or the institution for and in which I work. Instead, I have spent my time in the last 15-plus years seeking to understand the context, community and borough that I serve, without the need for affirmation. I have focused on achieving outstanding outcomes for all children that attend Mossbourne. We have achieved the best results for Black Caribbean boys in the country. In 2019, the last publicly available data at the time of writing, 79 per cent of Black Caribbean boys attending Mossbourne achieve 4+ in English and maths at GCSE, compared to 48 per cent nationally (ONS, 2022). Caribbean boys attending Mossbourne achieved on average a grade higher across all their subjects compared to their counterparts, with Progress 8 of -0.31 nationally compared to a Progress 8 of 0.81 at Mossbourne (ONS, 2022).

I have focused on working with others on anti-racism practices and education, in order to help bring about long-lasting and positive change. I have focused on creating safe and beautiful environments for our students, where they can achieve outcomes that many believe are not possible from children who live in areas of high deprivation. Yes, I seek to be understood now, after my years of learning, but my motivation is not to be gifted with any accolades or praise. I am very aware that this book is important for our community in Hackney and for our Hackney children.

For me, it is key that I maintain the freedom to do what is right so that I can take action where necessary, due to my awareness and knowledge of the context and structural limitations of the broader society that impact a person's ability to achieve. I'm very aware that if people, including leaders, are worried about job security, it can restrict them from doing what is right, and individuals often decide to take the 'safe' path rather than the right path as a result. I work and have worked in the London Borough of Hackney for over a decade, in one of the very few places across the world that is a true melting pot of people and culture, where every ethnicity, social class and faith reside. It is important for me to work with the community from a place of authenticity and mutual respect.

Although this chapter doesn't follow the format that you will see going forwards, I feel in that same vein that it is important for you to hear from somebody else as well, before I wrap this chapter up. Who better than Dipo, a man for whom I have the greatest respect and admiration? Like many COOs, he quietly goes about his role of keeping the federation afloat. He, along with many other COOs and key central team staff, is one of the unsung heroes of education – a person without whom we could not exist.

A word from Dipo Odunsi, Chief Operations Officer, The Mossbourne Federation

In my experience, one of Peter's qualities is that he is not afraid to take risks, even when it goes against popular opinion. When I joined Mossbourne I wasn't a member of the leadership team, and I recall a conversation with Peter within three months of my employment, during which he discussed extending my remit beyond finance and becoming a member of the leadership team. As I was new to the pre-college education sector, my initial reaction was to say no. However, I was reassured by Peter that not only do I have the qualities to be a good leader, but also that my work ethic is aligned with that of Mossbourne, and that he was going to guide me during the journey.

This quality of being able to take measured risks with staff (as in my case, and seen with other staff within Mossbourne and ProgressTeaching time and time again) or with key decisions impacting outcomes, is one of the reasons why Mossbourne is a successful trust.

In this book, Peter talks about exploring unfamiliar areas. What I find particularly significant about Peter's leadership style is his willingness to tackle challenging conversations, such as racism and the so-called underachievement of African and Caribbean pupils in the education system. While some senior leaders and headteachers shy away from acknowledging the reality that institutional racism exists and are prepared to excuse the failure of African and Caribbean pupils for reasons of poverty and other deprivation and upbringing excuses, Peter provokes leaders at Mossbourne into discussing these uncomfortable issues and into working collectively towards finding ways in which to remove barriers to achievement for these groups of pupils. I believe that this is a key factor in the stimulus for these groups of pupils to perform exceptionally well at Mossbourne.

What is truly significant about Mossbourne's success is that it is not a trust that pays lip service to putting the achievement of students at the front and centre of every decision-making process. Having worked in both public and private organisations, I sadly have to agree with Peter that sometimes leaders allow personal biases or the latest fad in education to distract from what is important – teaching, learning and empathy. He challenges leaders to do what is right – after all, that is what leadership is all about – and offers practical ideas and solutions that I know can work based on my own work experience and educational background.

Although my childhood background is very different from Peter's, I do recall that I was happiest when I was in school learning. Looking back, I attribute this to the relationship that I had with some of my teachers, who treated me with respect and provided me with self-esteem whenever it was needed.

It remains to be seen whether Ofsted will change its evaluation process, but I am certain that this book gives many useful strategies that leaders can adopt, not only to improve their engagement with pupils but also to improve and sustain outcomes.

Dipo Odunsi

Reflections

Throughout my career, I have never chased success; I've always just felt good about working hard due to my working-class background, and have prided myself on doing a good job. In fact, every time I've pushed for promotion, it hasn't worked. I have learned immensely from these knockbacks, and I hope that you will see how and why as you read about the rest of my journey throughout this book.

Among the other things that I've mentioned, I recognise that I am an immigrant from Oz. I am someone who has lived in England for over two decades and made it my home, but I haven't lost my accent (many would debate otherwise) and I haven't lost my absolute love to spin a yarn, which in Australia means to tell a story. I make no apology for telling stories about my experiences within each chapter, as I feel that these offer a chance to understand me and my leadership of the Mossbourne Federation, which is a huge part of my life. I hope that these insights help you to pinpoint the problems that you may have in front of you as you navigate your own career. They may help you to see the solutions more clearly. Being a leader in education is not easy, and my aim is that this book will give you the knowledge to develop the skills that you need, both known and unknown.

I have also come to realise that my life outside of the school setting offers a rich insight into leadership as well. Don't be alarmed when you encounter references to business theory and practice throughout this book. I became the CEO of an educational technology company (ProgressTeaching) as a result of my Executive MBA, and therefore I drip-feed this experience throughout the chapters as well. My rationale: if we are going to be different and change the face of education, we need to look outside of it for some of the answers.

A judgemental elephant

Aha. You've found one of the elephants in the room (aka book). Well done and no peeking to find out where the others are.

At this point, I think it would be fair to make a comment about Ofsted and inspection regimes. As someone working in the English system and writing a book about leadership, not addressing the elephant in the room would be a disservice. However, I promise that I won't refer to Ofsted very often within this book outside of this space and beyond this elephant ride.

I have been involved in many school inspections, some good and some bad, which is why it's important to acknowledge the high-stakes accountability structure within which all education leaders in England work. For me, the concept of inspections is an important and good one. I think that there should be inspections and some form of performance tables, but we can debate whether the current tables and inspection methodology measure what really matters. I don't think that they do. As I've said, I do feel that the concept of inspections is good and that they have their purpose, but I believe that they should work on a high-frequency, low-stakes model. We currently have some fundamental issues within the Ofsted inspection system:

- **The Chief Inspector:** At some point, we handed to a single person, the Chief Inspector, the ability to unilaterally decide what 'good' education in England looks like. This one person can, at will, change the inspections framework across England, causing a cascading impact throughout the whole system, only for it to be potentially changed again when their term in post is up (or before, if they change their mind) and the new Chief Inspector arrives to make their mark.

- **The lead inspector:** They are human. While some are objective and systematic in their approach, others present in very different ways. Some have a personal view that they bring overtly, some have a personal view that is unconscious and some just have a blatant preferred style that they expect to see. These four examples of lead inspectors could give four very different inspection gradings for the same school on the same day, which leads me onto the final key issue.

- **You can't challenge Ofsted:** Yes, you read that correctly and I'm aware that you technically can, but you just get nowhere. If you feel that your school has been wrongly judged and graded, you, as principal, can complain and appeal the decision. However, the only evidence that will be used during this process is the notes made by the inspectors during the school visit. I also need to point out that the person overseeing the investigation is a member of Ofsted. The icing on the Belgian bun is that, as the principal making the complaint (via letter and follow-up phone call) and appeal, you are not allowed to see the evidence from the inspection being used in the investigation. Whatever is written in the inspection notes is taken as gospel. All you have is your memory of the inspection, evidence shared by colleagues and your notes from meetings, including the end-of-day team meeting, if you have them.

From these points, it's easy to see the cracks in the fragmented accountability system that we continuously attempt to navigate. The Ofsted framework and handbook can be rewritten on what feels like a whim. At times, this has resulted in huge shifts of focus for Ofsted, such as the recent one from data to curriculum when the new Chief Inspector arrived on the scene in 2017. As well as this, Ofsted doesn't always sync with the views and needs of the Department for Education (DfE). All this being said, the commissioned research that Ofsted undertakes, both quantitative and qualitative, is generally positive if viewed through a case study lens, and has a place in the development of practices in education and the other areas that Ofsted oversees.

I want to highlight the fact that there are models available to study and adapt that could be used to quality-assure various aspects of schools. The one that instantly comes to mind is the financial audits that take place on a regular basis within schools with the Chief Financial Officer (CFO), their team and the audit committee. They ensure that there is compliance with the regulations that need to be adhered to, and that good practice is in place and followed. In the education sector and beyond, we've had a clear overview of what is expected of us and the audits of financial accounts for years. I believe that this transparent system should be mirrored for school inspections.

I'm sure that we can all agree that we should audit a system for many reasons, particularly those around safeguarding and for quality-assurance purposes. It is important that, as a public body, we are no different, and perhaps Ofsted should be the auditors instead of inspectors. What if, like an audit, schools either met expectations ('qualified' in financial accounts), either with or without recommendations, or did not meet expectations ('unqualified')? The use of recommendations would allow for a far more nuanced approach and provide schools with a concrete list of requirements. The recommendations could be split into:

- **urgent:** requiring immediate attention
- **important:** requiring attention at the earliest opportunity
- **routine:** action to be completed before the next audit.

In addition, auditors could highlight areas of good practice worth sharing with others. Schools could have, for instance, an audit cycle that closely mirrors the financial audits of:

- three internal audits a year (a model that many trusts already use)
- one external audit every two years, which focuses on the validity of the internal audits.

Internal audits would need to cover all aspects of school practice, including safeguarding, pastoral care, quality of education and leadership, but should have the flexibility to be extended to look at other items that the school deems important – sorry to use the Ofsted framework. For clarity, these would not replace the requirement for Ofsted or other bodies to undertake specific inspection when valid concerns are raised, such as around safeguarding of pupils. Schools could even be required to submit said reports to various bodies, such as Ofsted and the DfE, as is the case with financial audit reports, which are published at Companies House and on the trust's websites. School audits, like a financial audit, would be highly useful for management, governors, parents and other stakeholders. This high-frequency, low-stakes model would allow schools to focus on recommendations rather than the Ofsted grade.

We would need to be very careful with any agency created to conduct such audits, and those within education would most definitely need to be involved in what the focus should be if we are to avoid the system being at the whim of the current Chief Inspector. All systems need checks and balances, and no one should mark their own homework. For me, what is important is that we create a system that works for children, a system that encourages good leaders to take up headship and a system that has clarity on what 'good education' is.

2 Being mission-driven

Why are we here, in education? Why do you do what you do? This chapter looks at the underlying premise of educational leadership by explaining the 'why'. It is important to understand that if you are getting a group of people together, they need a focus. First we will look at the mission, and how easy it is to be distracted from it and knocked off course. The yarn explores the challenges that I faced as a new leader and how to ensure that you stay focused through planning, working methods, flow and collaboration. As the chapter moves into the key leadership skills of exploration and scrutiny, we dive into the key components of the creation of a MAT. I share frameworks that explain how to stay focused on the mission while creating a central services team and building a new school. You will be able to identify how to move from ideas through to actions and on to outcomes that have a positive and far-reaching impact on pupils and the school community. In this chapter's case study, I introduce you to Nick Rutherford, the founding principal of Mossbourne Victoria Park Academy (MVPA). My final thoughts on being mission-driven look at the importance of clear communication for a team and school culture.

The yarn

There is a lot of noise that can easily distract leaders from their core purpose and mission. We are, after all, in a sector heavily influenced by society and government policy, whether it be political unrest, ever-changing education secretaries, new initiatives or new research – the list is endless. This noise can be informative, like listening to Radio 4 (which is my favourite), but it can also become a blocker. My role as CEO in my organisation is to keep people on the right path towards the mission by ensuring that my principals and senior leaders can focus on the core purpose of teaching and learning, without being disturbed by the hubbub of the world around them.

Your mission needs to be explicit. My mission is clear: **we are changing children's lives for the better by creating an environment where learning is the norm**. Focusing on the mission is vital because it helps us to navigate a complex environment with many competing demands. Quite simply, if an initiative, idea or strategy doesn't fit the mission, why are we doing it? To sustain an exceptional school (or to create one in the first place), the mission needs to engender a following. My schools are unashamedly academic; however, this doesn't mean that we don't have happy children. Believe it or not, the two can go hand in hand and co-exist. For my team and me, it quickly became crystal clear that if we were going to change children's lives for the better, the default behaviour in our schools needed to be learning. If you can achieve this across your school (or group of schools, for that matter), you've cracked the nut; you've got an environment where learning is the norm. This sounds simple but it isn't, and sadly most leaders aren't even looking for it, especially in areas of high deprivation, where it is even more important. In my experience of going to school as a child and going into schools as an educator, the best learning took place in the classrooms where the default position was learning. Everything within those environments supported the individual child to achieve their best, build resilience and see the benefit of an education, irrespective of what barriers they faced.

Now once upon a time, I wrote a ten-year development plan, which I did use. It was on a double-sided A4 piece of paper; however, this is not something that I'm going to advocate or dwell on in this chapter. There are many books that will give you a proforma for your three-, five- or ten-year plan to work towards your mission, but this is not one of them. My only advice on this is to create one in a way that works for you and which you will use. Instead, I'm going to focus on how I became the principal of Mossbourne Community Academy (MCA) in 2012, after the widely known and respected leader Sir Michael Wilshaw left to become Her Majesty's Chief Inspector of Ofsted (2012–16). He had led the school from its inception in 2004 to 2011, taking it to great heights and doing what many believed was impossible for an inner-city London school located in Hackney. Prior to joining Ofsted, Sir Michael had a distinguished career as a teacher for 43 years, 26 of these as a headteacher in East London secondary schools and Executive Principal at MCA. In addition to leading MCA, Sir Michael was Director of Education for ARK, a charitable education trust running a number of academies across England.

Then I came along. I had nowhere near the same credentials. I'd worked in the school for several years already, and for a short time before Sir Michael's departure I had been the co-acting principal. The role came up for the substantive principal when Sir Michael was publicly named as the new Chief Inspector (see Rustin, 2011), and I had to decide whether I should apply. I spoke to my mentor at Future Leaders (now known as the Ambition Institute), a programme of which I'd been a part and which was formed to develop and support senior leaders in becoming headteachers in challenging schools (defined as those with over 30 per cent of children having free school meals). I also approached close, trusted friends for advice about the role and the prospect of leading such a renowned school, as I valued their thoughts and comments about putting myself forward for such a big opportunity.

All of them – every single one – asked me 'Why?' Why would I put myself into such a difficult position? Why would I even consider it? Why? Why? Why? The most compelling and profound comment of them all that comes to mind when I think back on this time was 'You are on a hiding to nothing' – a phrase that means that someone has absolutely no chance whatsoever of being successful. Evidently, my friends were adamant that they should give me the biggest, clearest warning they possibly could that applying for the role would be the biggest mistake of my life and career. They were extremely open and honest because they felt that if I was successful in getting the role, people would only ever attribute anything and everything that I did well to Sir Michael, and anything and everything that didn't go well directly to me. Basically, anything bad would go down as my own fault, label me a failure and be detrimental to my career. Quite frankly, I was being told by almost everyone that it was a lose–lose situation.

I am truly grateful for the friends and trusted work colleagues throughout my life who have given me their frank and sometimes brutally honest advice. These relationships are invaluable and essential to any leader. No one wants sycophants – 'yes men' (or women). I was and I am hugely thankful to them all. It's no secret, of course, that I applied for and got the job.

A close friend (who was and still is an exceptional principal and whom I admire greatly) told me jokingly for years after I took up the role that the results of the schools were not mine and they would, on an annual basis, as if a tradition to help to soften the blows from outside my circle of trust, attribute them to Sir Michael. What my trusted friends had predicted was true, of course; many in education outright refused to acknowledge that the exceptional results that continued to be achieved year in and year out were in any way influenced by anything that I had done.

The sixth year of my being in post came around and the ritual of the publishing of results took place as usual; however, this time it was different. I fondly recall my dear friend proclaim, while looking at and milling over the data (which, again, was exceptional), 'Sir Michael, Sir Michael who?' In their own way, they helped me to ride the waves of criticism and cynicism that had at times been relentless. There was now the acknowledgement from my peers that the prophecy of a lose–lose situation was, in fact, incorrect and that I had ultimately made the tough but right decision after all.

I am definitely not saying that the road was easy by any means, and many people have asked me, using a variety of phrases, 'Why be on a hiding to nothing?' It's a valid question. Something that has always stuck with me when asked and answering this question is this simple observation. I've seen this unfolding over the decades during which I have been working in education. To me, it feels as though many people want to be the hero leader; by this I mean that they are specifically focused on taking on schools judged as inadequate by Ofsted and making them good. It takes a certain type of leader and leadership to achieve this, and that is something that should never be underestimated or dismissed. However, on the other side of the spectrum, we have an ageing population of leaders, and the many, many great schools in which they have worked and that they have nurtured are in need of custodians. If the majority of leaders only focus on working in struggling schools and then moving on after making them great, what happens when they leave? We need to understand the moral purpose of taking on good and exceptional schools. Communities deserve consistency. The independent school sector prides itself on this: leaders are proud and excited to take on great schools such as Eton, St Paul's, Kings College, etc., with many of these principals staying in these institutions for decades. But who are the people in the state sector taking on great schools and keeping them there?

Sir Michael left at around the same time (give or take a few years) that Sir Alex Ferguson CBE left Manchester United. Ferguson was Manchester United's longest-serving manager (26 years) and is widely regarded as one of the greatest football managers of all time (clearly something that I can't admit as a Liverpool supporter), winning more trophies than any other manager in the history of football. Great football clubs need individuals to step up for the challenge of management, like great schools need individuals to step up for the challenge of leadership. There have been numerous high-profile leaders willing to take on Manchester United since Ferguson's departure, all with varying degrees of success. Yet when Sir Michael stepped down, only three leaders, including myself, put themselves forward for the role. Will you be the person to step up to the challenge of leading a great school? To me, Wilshaw felt like the Ferguson of education; there were no bigger personalities at the time. I'm pleased to say that I lasted longer than David Moyes (who followed Ferguson as manager of Manchester United from 2013 to 2014).

So why did I apply? In my short time in England, I had seen great schools come and go, like thieves in the night. It was a familiar pattern: the 'Super Head' arrives, the school gets some amazing outcomes, including an outstanding Ofsted, the leader moves on and the school quickly falls from grace, only for another school to take its place at the top of the tables. For me, the question was why this was not happening in England's long-standing public schools, like the Etons and Harrows of the world. Why have so many of England's institutions stood the test of time, like the livery companies in the City of London? The answer is simple. In these institutions, the institution itself is greater than any one individual or group of individuals. The leaders of these institutions are but custodians. I didn't want Mossbourne to be another fly-by-night school success, only to fade into the background when the Super Head left the building. What had been achieved – a school where learning was the norm, in every classroom, every day – was too important. In short, I was drawn to the mission – to continue it, and to be the next custodian of Mossbourne.

The brilliant thing about taking on an amazing school is that you have a great foundation on which to build. Within my first two years as the leader of Mossbourne, I:

- undertook and built a new secondary academy
- academised (and eventually turned around) a local failing primary school
- undertook and built a new primary academy
- formed The Mossbourne Federation MAT.

I'm aware that this sounds like sheer insanity for my first headship and progression into the role of CEO, but I was determined for more children to benefit from Mossbourne. To do this, we needed to build more schools for the community of Hackney where learning was the norm. But perhaps I'm mature enough now to admit that there was also just a little bit of ego and stupidity of youth at play as well.

My mission has and always will be focused on **changing children's lives for the better through creating environments where learning is the norm**. I could have easily been distracted and pulled away from this. You've read the CV of the man I followed to become principal. You've had a sense of the scrutiny that I received regarding the expectation of staying top of the results table, year on year, and seen the list of the numerous projects that I undertook within the first two years in post. Yet because of the great people around me, inside and outside of work, some of whom I have spoken about and some I will talk about later in the book, I was able to pull off what now seems like the impossible, and to stay focused on the mission: **to change children's lives for the better by creating an environment where learning is the norm**.

From Ofsted (2021, p. 2):

'What is it like to attend this school?

Mossbourne Community Academy changes pupils' lives for the better. The academy provides pupils with a far-reaching curriculum in and out of the classroom. Demanding rules and routines ensure that learning is front and centre at all times. Pupils are taught to aim high in order to reach their full potential. Pupils' exemplary behaviour means that teachers are able to teach and focus on learning. Pupils settle immediately so that no time is wasted. They listen, answer questions and get on with their work without fuss. As a result, pupils learn exceptionally well, achieve the highest results in examinations and leave school fully prepared for the next steps in their lives.'

I show this because, as much as we all have opinions – good, bad or indifferent – about Ofsted and the way in which it operates, we all love the feeling of a great comment from them, and we demonstrate this by posting them everywhere on our website, on banners around our schools and so on. External validation is important.

Leadership skills

Exploration: The action of exploring an unfamiliar area

It's easy to be put off by knock-backs but don't be. I like to describe myself as a pessimistic optimist. I'm a guy who sees the glass as half empty but can appreciate the fact that it's at least not completely empty. I guess this is my own version of the Stockdale Paradox, where I have the ability to navigate challenges while maintaining the belief that things will work out in the end. (The Stockdale Paradox is a technique to navigate challenging and ambiguous times through the ability to confront the brutal facts of your current reality even as you maintain unwavering faith that you will prevail in the end, no matter how distant that is – see ModelThinkers, 2022.) This has put me in a great position for the challenges that have been thrown at me unexpectedly in leadership.

In this section, I will explore how business models can be used to navigate some of the unexpected challenges when they are thrown at you. The mission for the trust was and continues to be **to change children's lives for the better,**

through creating environments where learning is the norm. My task was to take away the noise so that the principals could focus on the mission. This exploration into setting up a central services team for my MAT was important because I knew that doing this successfully would mean giving capacity back to the schools to focus on the mission. I'm aware that I could have easily used an example that focuses on teaching and learning, but I haven't. This book is different. I want to show you the elements of school leadership that go unseen and are not obvious. I want to challenge you to really consider the hidden elements that allow great teaching and learning to take place.

The danger of entering into such a big project is that it is very easy to be tipped off balance and lose focus on the mission. When you are in the quagmire, it's easy for the mission to be thrown out of the window and to believe that any solution will do. I was in a transition period that seemed to last forever. My role of new principal had quickly transformed to CEO because we were rapidly moving towards being an organisation consisting of four schools. I knew that I had to create a MAT, but I didn't have the know-how at the time. It was before I completed my Executive MBA, and this was also the period before it became commonplace to set up a trust. Creating the legal structure was the simple part; we contacted our solicitors, set the wheels in motion and that was that. However, what came after was a wicked problem that took greater time and consideration. Conklin and Weil (2007, p. 4) define a wicked problem as a problem with:

- no definitive definition
- 'an evolving set of interlocking issues and constraints'
- many stakeholders
- no final perfect solution.

Even as I write this, I am aware that many MATs – and businesses for that matter – are still trying to figure out the right balance between what is held locally (in a school) and what is held centrally. The answer to this question is whatever works best for your mission, your staff and ultimately your children.

Developing the MAT meant building an infrastructure that could work beyond that of an individual school. I needed to consider and build internal IT (information technology), finance, HR (human resources) and premises teams structures that could work successfully across the organisation. This experience of effectively building a whole new layer of a business, which worked as the brain of the organisation, was not only a key catalyst for me pursuing an MBA but also a great opportunity to create and build something that would continue the Mossbourne mission for all of its schools.

What do you do when there are no systems in place?

Sometimes when faced with a big challenge, it is extremely hard to figure out where to start; therefore, I hope that you benefit from the knowledge I've gained and that I wish I had to hand at the time. I knew that my core purpose was for my principals to have the time and mental capacity to be focused on what matters most: **changing children's lives for the better, through creating environments where learning is the norm**. I didn't want them being distracted by the noise of finance, IT, buildings, compliance, etc., which so many principals are pulled into, often to the detriment of teaching and learning. Therefore, we needed a central services team that would take ownership, in partnership with the principals, of the operational elements of the schools.

As we delve into project management frameworks, which are critical to building a MAT central services team, or supporting any substantial change for that matter, I want to first talk about the word 'agility'. Sheppard and Young (2006, p. 922) define agility as 'rapid whole-body movement with a change of velocity or direction in response to a stimulus'. As much as I would like to spend a few pages talking about agility in sport, I must get to the point. Agility – the ability to be agile, to rapidly change the pace or direction of your entire organisation – is critical and is something that is often lost as schools or MATs mature. Understanding the importance of agility and its implementation will allow you, as a leader, to keep your finger on the pulse of your organisation's development.

First introduced in the 1990s, the Agile Manifesto and philosophy came about as a response from a group of tech industry people to the limitations of traditional software development. The group of founders, Beck et al. (2001), wanted an approach to software development that emphasised flexibility, collaboration and incremental progress. Fast-forward over two decades, and the principles of the agile approach and frameworks to support it are found across multiple industries and are the preferred way of working on complex projects, due to the rapidly changing nature of the workplace in the twenty-first century.

Beck et al. (2001) state in their Agile Manifesto that they have come to value:

- **individuals and interactions** over processes and tools
- **working software** over comprehensive documentation

- **customer collaboration** over contract negotiation
- **responding to change** over following a plan.

While Beck et al. understand the value of the items on the right (e.g. process and tools), they believe that the items on the left (e.g. individuals and interactions) are more important in creating a better end product. For me, in this instance, the product was a central services team that allowed principals, teachers and support staff to focus on the mission.

Now at the time I was learning on the job, surviving off coffee and working 14-plus-hour days, living and breathing the creation of The Mossbourne Federation. My problem-solving and logical thinking skills got me through, but with my agile knowledge hat on and a good dose of hindsight, I can see where I fell short – but more on that later. The agile principles underpin multiple frameworks across multiple industries. They encourage iterative and incremental approaches that focus on delivering value to the customer or end user through collaboration, flexibility and adaptation to changing requirements and circumstances – a great set of principles to use when doing anything in education, which is such a mission-driven sector. It feels like Beck et al. could have easily written their values about education when they focused on the left-hand side:

- **individuals and interactions** becomes relationships over processes
- **working software** becomes doing what works for children over creating the perfect policy
- **customer collaboration** becomes working with all stakeholders over fighting against them
- **responding to change** is the life blood of education.

The agile principles provide a way of working, one that allows you to focus on your mission, relationships (more in Chapter 7), children and stakeholders, while responding to the changing needs of the educational landscape. However, when tackling a project, one also needs a framework. The framework that I will use in this chapter is one often used in software development, and breaks a project down into the following smaller and smaller components (see Figure 1):

1. Theme: the strategic initiative
2. Epics: the major areas within the strategy

3. User stories: an end goal expressed from the user's perspective

4. Task: a specific piece of work needed to achieve a user story.

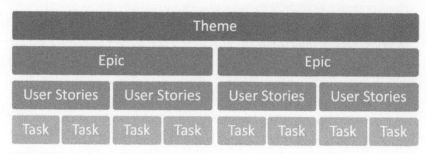

Figure 1

I use this not because it is perfect. There are many other frameworks that could easily be used to create a central services team. For that matter, one could use a simple action plan, something that I have seen used to great effect over the years. I select this framework because it forces you to think about the end user (staff and people) and the mission, something that I forgot to do in at least one part of our project to create a central services team. We definitely put process over individual users.

For me, when I think about applying 'agile', I think about it in three distinct parts. The first is the framework (Figure 1), which provides a process in which to work that offers comfort and reassurance. When working with a wicked problem, having a framework frees up mental capacity because we are not thinking of the 'how' but instead focusing on the 'what'. You don't need to have all the answers to start. You can focus on the first task: first things first. The second part is having the right people and doing the right things at the right time. Finally, when applying an agile philosophy, you must put the end user (a person) at the heart. I'm embarrassed to say that when setting up the MAT central services team, this part of the process wasn't always thought about.

Embracing a framework

Obviously, I had my theme:

> *To create a central team in order for my principals to have the time and mental capacity to be focused on **changing children's lives for the better, through creating environments where learning is the norm**.*

And I knew what was needed in terms of my epics. For example, in finance:

To develop a single finance function that meets people's needs for ordering, payroll, pension and other internal requirements, while at the same time remaining compliant, allowing us to pass an audit and demonstrate good financial management of public funds.

What we didn't know were the user stories. It's OK not to know. You need to talk to people and understand their requirements. You only need one story to start. For example, let's use the ordering process in a school:

'As the site manager, I want to register that an order has arrived, so that it can be delivered to the right department.'

The first user story often leads to the second:

'As the head of department, I want to confirm that an order is complete so that finance can release payment.'

And the second to a third:

'As the head of department, I want to let finance know that an order is incomplete, so that the remaining items can be chased up and only part payment released.'

User stories often quickly cascade as the project unfolds. All will work, as long as the theme and epics are clear and you are willing to iterate 'trust the process'. What was helpful for me was asking a few crucial questions throughout.

- Can the system/s in place handle multiple schools?
- Will it meet the basic requirements for scrutiny?
- Should it be operated locally (school), centrally (trust) or hybrid?

And I should also have asked: Does this meet the end user's requirements?

There will be some trial and error, of course; nothing is a perfect science. As someone who is extremely logical in my thinking, I can also acknowledge that one needs to be flexible and add emotional intelligence into the mix. Taking calculated risks (I talk more about this in Chapter 4) is part of the process.

The people

Ultimately, the role of project manager, for building the trust central services team, fell to me. I was the person who was going to make sure that everything that needed to be completed got completed. But I also had to identify my key players (or start the process of recruitment if I didn't have them) who would oversee each area of the operation. It is advisable to consider that some individuals struggle when moving to a central MAT structure from an individual school. Never presume that someone who is highly effective at school level operations can transition to MAT-level operations with ease or that they would even want to. The same could be said for the people that can move a school from 'requires improvement' to 'good' or 'outstanding'. They are key players in a team but are not necessarily the people who can keep a great school great. Becoming great and maintaining great are two different journeys.

A user-centric approach

Having now been exposed to the positives and negatives of the tech world, specifically the development of educational software, I've come to understand that great pieces of technology have the user at their centre and are solving a problem that the user wants solved. Additionally, technology or software companies often talk about the user experience. It's not enough to solve the problem; we need to do it in a way that has maximum benefit to the user with minimal – if any – pain. Being truly honest, I know that originally, during this huge learning curve for me and my team, we didn't focus on the people who would be using the software and systems (the end users). We focused on compliance, especially in finance. We implemented systems that auditors loved but that didn't support HR, payroll or the people managing orders.

A huge spotlight was shone on our non-user-centric approach when, during my MBA, I was tasked with an assignment to 'review a business process', map it out, understand how it worked and make recommendations for its improvement. I chose my trust's ordering system because it had had numerous complaints ever since its rollout. My analysis found that the process contained four of the seven service wastes: unclear communication, unnecessary movement, duplication and incorrect inventory (with the others being delays, errors and opportunities lost – Lean Manufacturing Tools, 2017). In total, I found no less than 18 different recommendations for improvement, ranging from duplication of tasks to managers and operators who had completely different views on how the system worked. In short, the people in the process were constantly working around its limitations.

The review process was cathartic and showed me:

1. the importance of placing the users at the heart of any decision to procure software or create or implement a new process or policy

2. that one should never assume that leaders, including oneself, know how something works in practice, no matter how vehemently they tell you (or you tell yourself)

3. that leaders should try, at least once, to unpick a process in its entirety. It's incredibly valuable as a leader, even as a CEO, to realise how processes in your organisation actually work, rather than how you imagine that they work.

Friends who work in hotel management have said to me that the hotel industry trains its managers by getting them to do all the jobs in the hotel for a short period of time. This provides managers with a unique understanding of how their hotel functions and what it truly takes to make it work. I feel that education has something to learn from this model. Often, we think that because we have taught, we know everything that there is to know about making a school work. Nothing could be further from the truth. I have to be honest: I fell into the quagmire, rolled around and covered every inch of myself in the joyous oozy mud. I believed wrongly in one area (I have to say only one of many) that the solution was fit for purpose when it wasn't! But the beauty of the agile philosophy and good leadership is that you go back, review and stress-test your thinking against the reality. Through the lens of my assignment, we were able to unpick the factors that were not working, change them and, in the process, learn a great deal. The daily challenge is staying focused on the mission. It is and always will be the job.

You might be wondering how all this relates to being mission-driven. Quite simply, every time a process or a policy or an infrastructure in your organisation doesn't have the user and the mission at the centre, you are being distracted from the mission. So I tell this story deliberately because it's not the obvious choice. It's one about which many will ask, 'What does this have to do with the mission? It's insanity!' It's easy to think about the mission in relation to teaching and learning, but they are not the only parts that make up a school. Have you ever wondered what a principal, CEO or CFO does all day? Be honest – you have, because most of it (if done well) you don't notice. This is a look behind the curtain, after all.

Scrutiny: Critical observation or examination

There is no greater test of a school's mission than expansion. I'm not talking about the kind of expansion where you grow from a two-form-entry primary to a three-form one; I'm focusing on the type of expansion where you are building a school from scratch. I've spoken about the development of the central services team and how that can put a strain on staying focused on the mission. But to take your mission, a plot of land and a Grade II listed building and create a brand new secondary school – now that is a challenge that will test your ability to hold true to the mission.

We have a mission: **To change children's lives for the better by creating an environment where learning is the norm**. I have repeated it throughout this chapter deliberately. Have you got it yet? You can immediately sense a school where learning is the norm. It's a school where teaching comes first. It's a school where teachers can teach and children can learn uninterrupted by poor behaviour. It's a school where it is cool to learn. It's a school where system and processes are effective and are designed to promote teaching. It's a resource-rich, clutter-free and clean environment that promotes teaching and learning. In short, it is an environment where nothing is more important than teaching and learning. However, when parents, pupils, the community and many teachers think of a school, they often think of the artefacts (the by-products) of our mission. The artefacts are the tangible outcomes. They may even be listed as your key performance indicators (KPIs).

Mossbourne artefacts include:

- GCSE outcomes in the top one per cent in the country
- a rowing team who have rowed at Henley, among other regattas, one of the best-known regattas in the world
- students annually finishing our sixth form and going on to read at Oxford and Cambridge colleges
- students attending school daily in award-winning buildings designed for their learning
- the primary children year in, year out achieving above national outcomes
- all primary pupils learning an instrument
- an endless list of medical students who are now NHS doctors
- students attending university in the USA.

I could continue, but I need to stop bragging now. Artefacts are great to help others – and yourself for that matter – to visualise the mission, but they should never be mistaken for the mission. Once we had established and codified what makes Mossbourne Mossbourne (the essence of the mission and values), the cycle of perpetuated success was born – well, with a great deal of focus and energy on staying true to the mission. This is not a self-perpetuating engine, after all. Our mission at The Mossbourne Federation means providing our children with an education on a par if not better than that provided by the best private schools. I want the name 'Mossbourne, Hackney, London' on a CV to mean something – the same as Eton does. I believe that the mission has to be bigger than you if you are to succeed. Eton outlives its principals. I wanted Mossbourne to be bigger than any one principal as well. It's what the community of Hackney deserves. Being a 'brand' in which people trust has more longevity than a brand focused on a single person. Mossbourne will be around in 100 years, long after I'm gone, and it will continue to mean success, as anything less is not even a consideration for the governing body, for the community or for the children, who all know what they are worth: the very best.

The focus in this section is on the importance of a building and the role that it can play in supporting the mission. This is especially true when the mission is **creating an environment where learning is the norm**. As described earlier, it's easy to be bumped off task and create any solution rather than walk the often-challenging path to stay true to the mission. In this section, I will scrutinise how, through critical observations, we were able to navigate and overcome the difficulties that we encountered on this endeavour.

The building of Mossbourne Victoria Park appeared to have all the stars aligned for success from the outset:

- There was a need for a school in the local area.
- The local community wanted a school.
- The local authority wanted the school and were even willing to provide the land.
- The government acknowledged the need for a school in the area and wanted to fund it.
- All parties concerned wanted Mossbourne to operate the school.

How difficult could it be to renovate a Grade II listed school building and add additional space to accommodate the four-form-entry school (equating to 120 per year group) that needed to be built?

I quickly realised that everyone wanting a school didn't necessarily mean that everybody could agree on the how, what or where. Discussions with architects, kickbacks on the design from locals and mountains of red tape to cut through meant that the original goal of building a school to support a growing community at times looked impossible.

There were two concerns from the community:

- They wanted a school, but a small village one and not a large comprehensive.
- They didn't want the new buildings overshadowing (and destroying) their gardens.

The community (a small vocal minority, at least) were worried about the volume of children that the new academy would bring and the new single building (offering passive supervision) blocking out the sunlight into their gardens and the impact on their way of living. Following these concerns, I found myself one afternoon sitting in another meeting, where I was being told again all the things that we couldn't do. Take a moment to imagine a group of architects and builders pointing to a map of the site, saying: We can't build here because of the protected trees. We can't build here because the site is too small. We can't build here because the residents have objected. We can't build here because of the residents' right to light. We can't build here because of National Heritage restrictions. It was slowly dawning on me that unless we did something different, we would have to forego our desire for a single additional building and our stated intent to maximise passive supervision.

For the uninitiated, passive supervision is where any teacher, teaching assistant, adult or pupil is constantly able to see (supervise) what is happening around the school. One classic example of this is having glass walls or doors on offices and classrooms. This allows teachers in offices to see in the corridor without needing to get up from their work – they can passively supervise the corridor. For clarity, this passive supervision does not extend to lesson changeover, but it does highlight – and this is a critical idea – the fact that the buildings that we use and in which we learn are important. The important role that buildings can play in the culture of a school never really gets mentioned, nor how the design of a school can actually make teachers' lives easier. Teaching is already a hard job; we don't need buildings to make it any harder. The second example of passive supervision that you may have encountered is a single playground space with no hidden corners between or behind buildings, allowing full visibility of children while not in lessons. Both examples significantly reduce things like inappropriate behaviour and bullying with minimal input, therefore contributing to the creation of an environment where learning is the norm.

So, taking you back to the meeting room with people pointing at a map, all of whom were aware of the difficulties but had never run schools themselves, I hope that you can understand why it wasn't as straightforward as me saying to the group, 'Do the best you can do, and we will make it work.' Sometimes, the attention to detail is everything. To compromise at that point would have impacted on the learning environment of all children and staff attending the school for decades to come. Let me say that again: for decades to come. We needed to think 'outside the box' and find a solution. I could rapidly feel the room being bumped off task. Suggestions of multiple smaller buildings were being aired. I knew that passive supervision was essential to the mission, which was best achieved with the addition of a single multi-storey building. Anything else would have led to a compromise. Multiple smaller buildings meant more hidden spaces, with greater opportunities for bullying and negative behaviour.

No one had considered building on the dead-end road to the side of the school site, which had no houses on it. So I raised the question: why don't we just build it on the road? I had a good relationship with the council, who wanted and needed the school to be built. The question was debated and after a few meetings the council agreed to close the road and cover the costs of diverting the services (electric, gas, etc.) that ran down the centre of the unused road. This allowed us to close the road and build the proposed building in its place. You often have to pick your battles, but it is still important to recognise when the situation is too important to compromise on. Don't compromise when you can see the benefits for children; it may involve being creative and finding an alternative way to achieve your mission, but that's OK. Try not to be the person who looks for the quickest and easiest way out. It is your role to hold the line and work with your team to come up with, or search for, the idea that allows the mission to flourish.

I can hear you asking, 'Did you just take a road and build your school on it?' Yes we did – a beautiful, award-winning one at that. Sometimes you need to ask for the earth because you might just get it. I guess that's how we were able to shut down a road in the middle of London to build a beautiful space for children to learn. Mossbourne Victoria Park's award-winning (2016 finalist for the Best Education Project at the Structural Timber Awards – Jestico + Whiles, 2023) single building, the Carol Building, is named after Veronica Carol,

MCA's first deputy principal. Veronica was the magic and driving force behind making the vision the reality. It is thanks in no small part to her that the Carol Building was and is able to support the mission. I recall sitting down with Veronica, with the proposed architectural plans laid out on the table in front of us, as we started the task of considering how the placement of every office, classroom and toilet would impact the passive supervision and, ultimately, the Mossbourne mission.

I have no doubt that this focus on **changing children's lives for the better by creating an environment where learning is the norm** helped MVPA to create artefacts of its own, such as:

- GCSE outcomes in the top one per cent in the country
- an annual science fair
- strong links with local businesses
- students who are a part of the Mossbourne rowing team who have rowed at Henley, among other regattas, one of the best-known regattas in the world
- students who have gone on to read at Oxford and Cambridge.

Case study: Nick Rutherford, founding principal of MVPA (secondary), England

Introduction

I first met Nick in September 2009, when he joined MCA as Head of Learning Area for English from Ifield Community College in Crawley. If you have ever had the joy of meeting Nick, you will know what I mean when I say that he exudes his passion for English. I guess this is no surprise given that he was drawn to teaching by the thought of having the same impact on children that his English teachers had on him. Nick took on the challenge of being the founding principal of MVPA in 2014. Under Nick's leadership, MVPA achieved GCSE outcomes in the top one per cent. What follows is that story.

Mossbourne Victoria Park Academy opened in September 2014. As was common for start-up schools in the noughties and beyond, the buildings weren't quite finished in time, so I delivered my opening address on the first inset day in a hard hat. I spoke to the 12 teaching staff and eight support staff about the mission, and we spent those first days carefully planning for the arrival of our first cohort of 120 Year 7 students.

We had been given the task of opening 'another Mossbourne' following MCA, which had been, was and still is one of the most talked-about, visited and successful secondary schools in the country. It was also a chance to prove the power of 'the Mossbourne Way'. One of the criticisms that had always irked me when I worked there was that the first school's success had been down to high levels of funding. It certainly had been given high levels of funding – a Richard Rogers-designed building and huge amounts of start-up capital. But my feeling had always been that it was the ethos, the expectations and the culture that had made it all work. And now, as we opened under the austerity coalition, with the same funding agreement as everyone else, we had the chance to prove it.

The crucial thing was not to copy. Although only a couple of miles from central Hackney, South Hackney was a different community with its own character. A copy-and-paste school wouldn't have the flexibility to serve that community, so it was important to separate the principles from the visible behaviours. But at its core, the mission **to change children's lives for the better by creating an environment where learning is the norm** was clear. All children have the potential for academic excellence. Not national averages. Not meeting expectations. Excellence.

At first, it was like a strange reality TV show. With only 12 teaching staff, we did everything together – always on duty, all teaching in the part of the building that was finished, all doing at least three assemblies in the year, all planning and delivering lessons in at least two subjects – and all aware that these first 120 students were crucial. Get it right with them, and they would model it for the successive year groups. Mess it up and we might never get it back.

So everything mattered. A child muttering under their breath after being reprimanded was a huge deal. If a student wasn't doing their homework, I knew about it. Parents who had got used to primary schools who didn't always follow through with what they said had to be shown that we were different. It was intense, and occasionally staff commented that we would never keep up the attention to detail with two, three or four year groups, at which point I would give them my analogy about shallots.

Well – not shallots exactly. French sauces in general. Lots of classic French sauces are made mostly with stock. But huge amounts of work go into making an initial base: shallots in butter married with strong flavours, vinegars or wine, herbs and spices, aromatics and oleaginous tinctures, building up a deep, intense base. And even though you then dilute it with stock so that the flavours became more subtle, the structure and character of the sauce lives in that original, overly intense beginning. That was us, I kept saying. In terms of behaviour, we let nothing go. With teaching and learning, we observe each other teach all the time and hold each other to account. For CPD (continuous professional development), safeguarding, curriculum – everything was done with an attention to detail that we knew we could never sustain because, as new staff and new students joined the school, and as the intensity of the first year was inevitably diluted, the standards that we set in that first year would be in the DNA of the school.

In many ways, year two was the biggest challenge, as the school doubled in size. We took on ten new staff and welcomed another year group. Over-communication was key: 'low-threat, high-challenge' conversations had to be held every day, and it was in that year that I realised how big a sales job being a headteacher was. Not just to students and parents – that was the same sales pitch that every teacher has to do, about why education matters and why it is, in the end, in the child's best interests to work with the school rather than against it – but to staff. It was, of course, a challenge constantly selling the mission, explaining the 'why' over and over again, so many times that I got sick of hearing my voice saying it. It was mentally exhausting ensuring that I was always being intentional in my use of language. I had to ensure that I was being careful to model the expectations and the vision in every conversation with a student or parent. And I made mistakes – glorious, huge, life-affirming mistakes that I recommend to everyone – but I generally managed to spot them, reverse them and, where necessary, apologise for them. That's important – it's so easy to get into a bunker mentality when you're doing something the hard way, but I actually think that that makes it even more important to constantly consider whether you might be wrong.

This, by about year four, had turned into one of my favourite phrases: 'flexible rigidity'. Coined by my incredible vice-principal, it captured something really important about being mission-driven: that the mission itself must be an organic thing, which is allowed a level of freedom to change and grow. The core purpose of excellence never changed, but we all learned so much about when to stand firm and when to let things evolve. When the first results came, the school was comfortably in the top 100 nationally for progress, and was recently (under my former incredible vice-principal, and now the head) rated as outstanding in all areas under the current Ofsted framework. That the mission was accomplished was down to the same thing as the success of any school – the remarkable, inspirational work of staff and students. But it was the sense of mission towards which we worked, in which we genuinely believed, and which we came to understand as an organic, responsive thing itself that made the difference.

The solution

Ensure that you understand that mission-driven means that you run your organisation in pursuit of said mission.

1.   Be clear about who you are as an organisation and stick to it. Unity.

2.   Be unapologetic but not closed when it comes to challenge, whomever it comes from. No excuses.

3.   Reflect, question and think deeply but don't flinch in your pursuit of excellence.

Your mission is a worthy pursuit, but not necessarily a clear or easy one, so invite people in. We all need critical friends, quality assurance and fresh eyes. Mission-driven leaders make day-to-day decisions that are aligned with their values. They create a path on which the team will follow them, because they all believe in the organisation's values and seek to know and contribute to the world beyond themselves. Yet quite often, a mission-driven life is challenging.

The pursuit of exceptional is rewarding, sure, but it is often fraught with struggle and relentless work, and can be downright exasperating.

The final words

If I were to condense mission-driven into just one word, it is to *strive* – a word that, by definition, requires an expenditure of great energy and effort. But I also believe that mission-driven individuals and organisations should be able to thrive. Don't forget to celebrate the wins and successes along the way.

Organisations that are mission-focused and -driven are more likely to be optimistic and confident about the future. This is because there is a strong sense of purpose that's defined by a genuine commitment to the social good, which is embedded throughout the organisation. The secret to high-performance organisations is that there is a high level of trust. It makes a lot of sense that if people can see proof – that they're visibly making a difference to the pupils and school as a whole – then they will trust the leadership decisions when they arise, as the motives are transparent.

Understanding the importance of actively involving all stakeholders, while at the same time communicating how each individual's contribution relates to the outcome, is an art form and a key skill. Organisations with established high-functioning workplace cultures are those who have an authentic and well-communicated mission. When crafting a clear school focus, including both the 'how' and the 'why' enables senior leaders to collectively focus their staff through a shared understanding and acceptance of the mission. It's much easier to communicate and direct behaviour, as well as guide strategic decision-making, when everyone is clear on the goal.

Top tips

- Be clear about the mission and be unwavering in your determination to achieve it.
- Artefacts are a great way in which to share your mission, to help people and to visualise what you want. What are your artefacts?
- Know the why: why are you doing this? What is your purpose?
- The mission is everywhere, and not just in obvious places like pastoral support, and teaching and learning.

3 Doing what is right, not what is popular

Being popular is not something of which I've often been accused – in my career at least – but I've learned to be OK with that. I've learned that the path of leadership often leads down the road less travelled.

This chapter looks at the concept of people-pleasing. Trying to please all of the people all of the time doesn't work. Having a strong sense of belief in where you are going is vital, but not everyone will agree with it or want to follow you. Some may even try to sabotage your efforts. The key driver for success must be the mission and its artefacts. For us, these artefacts are academic outcomes and opportunities for all. To achieve this, a school needs to focus on establishing a set of standards based on the mission and sticking to them. You need to be able to identify when things are wrong, realise it quickly and change. The key leadership skills focused on in this chapter are based around analysis and research examples, because the use of data to inform leadership decisions is a powerful and often underutilised tool. I'll also introduce you to Stephen Hall, the CEO of Camden Learning, and discuss his experiences of knowing the right paths to take in leadership decisions. My final thought on doing what is right and not what is popular looks at the importance of collecting and analysing the information that you have to hand, alongside what is in the best interest of the children in your school or MAT.

The yarn

You may find this yarn a little challenging to read, so please accept this as a trigger warning, but I also want you to remember as you read it that it all worked out OK, as I'm sitting here writing this book and leading a good and happy life. During this chapter in my life, there were great costs felt and there were also enormous benefits but, ultimately, I believe that I made the right decision to live with my adopted family.

By the end of my time in Year 5, it was clear that my parents had finally made the right decision to split for good. It didn't end harmoniously, which I'm sure isn't a surprise. There is never a good time for turbulent relationships to end, but I do wish that it hadn't been Christmas Eve. As a result of their turmoil, we three children found ourselves alone the night before Christmas without a parent in sight. My big brother – my idol – had the tenacity to lead my little sister and me to the only place of safety that we knew at the time: our grandma's. She lived some several miles away. On Christmas Eve, after realising that we were alone with no awareness of when or whether anyone would be coming back, my big brother took charge. He made the difficult decision to take us from the place of uncertainty and lead us along the highways and byways to grandma's.

As with any parental break-up – and this wasn't our first – a child's life becomes very different overnight. We didn't stay at grandma's for long. After the split, dad moved in with his old flame, whom he eventually married, and I went to live with them. My sister joined after a short period of time. But my brother Andrew and I never lived under the same roof again. I sometimes think about my big brother over this period. He became lost to us during this time. He floated in and out of spaces, never really settling in one place. I often wonder whether his life would have been different had my father taken him in as his own. Andrew never knew – none of us did – who his father was.

My sister and I began to settle into a new routine, of seeing our mum and living mainly with our dad and step-mum. At the beginning of Year 9, I got chickenpox and I recall missing more time from school. However, when I returned, things were different this time. I guess that I was different. It was the only period in my life when I didn't like school. I didn't even want to be in my maths classes, which everyone knows is my happy place. School wasn't my safe spot anymore. In Sydney, Australia, schools are big, busy places and I got lost. I'd fallen behind and couldn't keep up or understand what was happening in my lessons. I distinctly remember a time in my maths class where I just could not get factorising quadratic trinomials (double brackets) and feeling more and more frustrated with myself and the lesson. Sometimes children fall apart, and no one notices.

Things took another big turn when my step-mum's son returned after being away. There wasn't room for us anymore. Dad, my sister and I were kicked out. There was no choice but for us to be split up again. My little sister went first to stay with family friends, later moving on to stay with our mum in Yass and finally to our grandma's in Sydney. I was whisked away from the big city to the little town of Quandialla, to live with another friend of the family. I had never been away from my little sister for such a long period of time, and I felt it. We of course visited each other, but it wasn't the same and time became fragmented again.

When I arrived at my new school, the principal gave me a good once-over. As I'd come from the 'big city', they presumed wrongly that I was going to be trouble and told me very clearly, 'We don't fight here.' In a small town of under 500 people, I was put into a class of nine children (that's right – there were only nine students in Year 9, my year group) and I excelled. Miss Pirera, my maths teacher, among other teachers, was the sustenance that brought me back to life and allowed me to find my safe place again in school. She saw that I was exceptional at maths, had high expectations of me and was able to give me the support that I needed. She reignited my love for maths again as a result of her care and attentiveness. This was also the space where I became friends with Dallas (who would become my brother) and met the family who would ask me to choose them.

This yarn comes back to another Christmas and also to the point where I focus on doing what is right and not what is popular. I'm 14 now, and it's the end of Year 9. I was regularly visiting my mum and sister in Yass and, believe it or not, I even had a girlfriend there. My mum had been talking to me on and off during my visits about moving to be with her and my sister. Thoughts about the possibilities kept running through my mind, as my little sister felt like home and always has done. It was tempting and the pull was there, leading me to that decision, but something happened.

Back in Quandialla, my good friend Dallas invited me to his house (not that I needed an invite) to join their family meeting. I thought nothing of it; I'd practically lived in their home and in their lives every day for months like family. When I arrived and sat down, they told me that they were planning to move to Young. It was at this point that my since-adopted mum asked me whether I wanted to come and live with them.

I was 14. I had to make a life-changing choice and couldn't stop ruminating about the possibilities. My heart was being pulled towards my mum and my sister in Yass: the familiarity of what I knew, the love for my little sister and the excitement of a first girlfriend. But my heart was also being pulled towards a mum who had shown me what security looked and felt like. A family who had whole-heartedly offered me stability, warmth, boundaries and laughter, where I had been given the opportunity to understand that love could be freely given without any expectation or payment. To say that it was an impossible choice to make is an understatement. **I was 14.**

But sometimes in the stillness, when the thoughts give way for a moment, there is clarity. Sometimes you have to do what is right and not what is popular, and be prepared to own the choice that you make. I chose the right thing for me: I chose to give myself a chance and move to Young with my adoptive family.

Doing the right thing may initially sound simple, but it can be very difficult to practise. The phrase 'doing what is right, not what is popular' evokes memories from different stages of my career, but for me it is most akin to being a radical. It often feels that doing the right thing, for children, is radical. Bear with me as I elaborate.

A year into my role as principal, I found myself talking to a parent who had returned to the school to attend one of our annual community events. Her son, who was autistic, had left the school the previous year to attend a local college. I, of course, asked her how he was getting on and her stark response surprised me. It highlighted the impact that a school (or, in this case, a college) can have on young people by putting a limit on what they can reach. She informed me that her son's experience within the first six months had not been good, as it had taken the college this period of time to realise that he could read fluently and independently and loved it.

You see, the college set a limit on this young man's capacity to achieve and learn, because they prioritised his diagnosis of autism and used it as an obstacle to the possibilities that should have been afforded to him. During his time in my school, he had enjoyed and benefited from being in an environment that offered him sustenance for his hidden talents. We nurtured, challenged and pushed him to be the best that he could be with no limits but, upsettingly, when it was time for him to leave secondary and enter into the 'real' world, he was reduced to a label, which included low expectations.

My school's values, which we live and breathe, are 'Excellence, No excuses and Unity'. We are radicals and proud of this fact, because we notice every child and we use every resource available to us to try to catch them before they could ever fall. We understand the world from which some of them come. And we are by no means alone in this endeavour.

As part of the Future Leaders programme I was introduced to Doug Lemov and the amazing work that he was doing in America through the Uncommon Schools Network (https://uncommonschools.org), loosely based on the KIPP model (www.kipp.org). I was on the Future Leaders programme at the time. He had created the Teach Like a Champion framework, which was made into a book of the same name (2010).

Prior to Lemov there had been no shortage of suggested solutions for the 'poor performance that plagued the American school system' (Green, 2010). Many believe that the issue was instruction, including Lemov. However, he didn't prescribe to the widely held belief at that time that great teachers had something special: they had the 'it' factor. Sylvia Gist, the dean of the college of education at Chicago State University was quoted in the *New York Times Magazine* (Green, 2010) as saying 'I think that there is an innate drive or innate ability for teaching'. Lemov's view, that what we saw when watching great teachers was well-crafted, highly honed practice, was radical. He was saying that the challenges being faced in the education system existed in the classrooms, and that the exceptional teachers he was observing were the experts who held the answers. It wasn't a popular approach at the time: teaching being something that could be codified and taught was considered radical. Lemov's role was to find great teachers, study them and share what they did, in order for others to copy, practise and adapt for their own teaching. He was bold and approached a problem (that many were ignoring) differently. When he shared this study, the programme and its results resonated with people globally and his book sold worldwide.

In another period in my life, I witnessed the ongoing rhetoric of negativity regarding the high aspirations that Sir Michael had for pupils who attended a school in the heart of Hackney. Many wanted to see the school fail and not achieve the goals that it set for itself. People couldn't understand why he kept proclaiming that he could make the impossible happen in an area where low aspirations were the norm. I realise now that he was seen as rocking the boat and as a radical.

I'm drawn back home to a news article about a Queensland professor who was inspiring Year 6 students to study rocket science. The professor was thinking outside the box, ruffling feathers and aspiring for something great for the community. CQUniversity's Dean of Research, Professor Steven Moore, proposed a space research centre at CQU Mackay Ooralea to increase interest in the space industry (Wykeham and Maidson, 2020). It would give students opportunities to learn about satellite development, science, technology, engineering and mathematics (STEM) education, remote sensing applications and communications. Moore wanted to bring a love of STEM and industry to his community and was seen as a radical.

All three examples – Lemov, Sir Michael and Professor Moore from Oz – demonstrate the same core belief that we set the limits that we can achieve. Often people will attempt to put limits not only on themselves but also on others. **Sometimes you have to do what is right and not what is popular, and be prepared to own the choice that you make.** We at Mossbourne choose the right things for our children in our community, to give them a chance to move to places beyond their wildest dreams. Doing the right thing may initially sound simple, but it can be very difficult to practise.

Leadership skills

Analysis: Detailed examination of anything in order to understand it

Education in the London Borough of Hackney had undergone a significant transformation since 2002, with the opening of seven new secondary schools and one new sixth form college. Originally, most of the secondary schools were not designed to have a sixth form provision. However, with the local sixth form college underperforming and the new secondary schools exceeding expectations, six of the seven new secondary schools had opened or planned to open a sixth-form provision.

For me, it made no sense for each of my secondary schools to have sixth forms. They were less than 3 km from each other and there was a significant surplus of sixth form places in Hackney, because each 11–16 school was opening its own sixth form. Funding cuts and teacher shortages (yes, we are still talking about the same issues in 2023 as we were in 2017) were making local sixth forms a non-financially viable option. The challenge of filling sixth forms across the borough was having an adverse impact on budgets and, in turn, on the provision. Mossbourne was no different. I knew that opening a second sixth form in this environment was irresponsible. Two sixth forms were a risk – a high one at that – which would not benefit our community. What is right is often at the mercy of what is popular. In this case, there was significant pressure both internally and externally to open a second sixth form at MVPA. I needed to formulate a plan.

The focus in this section is on the importance of analysis in order to understand something, especially if you are entering new territory. Making a decision regarding the big step of further developing the sixth form needed a robust plan – one that could demonstrate the benefits and be difficult to disagree with.

At the time, we already had a sixth form in place that was operating in a market where supply (capacity) far outstripped demand (uptake). The sixth-form market in Hackney was saturated. In September 2016, 27 per cent of 1,550 places went unfilled (Hackney Learning Trust, 2017a). The market capacity was set to increase to 1,910 places by 2022. If the relationship between the number of places in Hackney (note: not all places in school-based sixth forms in Hackney are filled by Hackney residents, nor do all Hackney residents attend Hackney sixth forms), as measured by the Greater London Authority (2017), and the number of students accepting places in Hackney school-based sixth forms (Hackney

Learning Trust, 2017b) continued to track Hackney's population, then, despite population growth, a significant surplus of places would remain (see Figure 2 on the next page).

In order to understand where all the challenges were, I first needed to review three broad strategic areas: the geographical scope, the product market and the vertical scope.

- **The geographical scope:** We mainly attracted Hackney children to our sixth form due to our locality. We did have the option of looking more widely, but if other issues were addressed first regarding the sixth form dilemma, this wouldn't need to be a priority.

- **The product market:** We were offering the same classes as other sixth forms in the area (A levels), but we did not offer vocational courses, which the others did. This wasn't something that I was looking at changing.

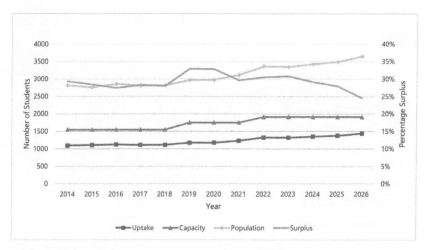

Figure 2 *Capacity against uptake in Hackney School based Sixth Form*

- **The vertical scope:** Vertical integration is a strategy that allows a company to streamline its operations by taking direct ownership of various stages of its production process, rather than relying on external contractors or suppliers (Hayes, 2022). I could quickly see that this was the area where we could have the greatest chance of success. We had a second secondary school and therefore a larger control than most over our vertical scope and the opportunities that it gave us to focus on changing children's lives for the better. It gave me some clear parameters within which I could comfortably work. I knew that we could only run one sixth form. We would also have to reduce the number of subjects on offer if the single sixth form was going to be viable. We needed to do something different and not just have a sixth form as a vanity project.

At the time, the sixth form's capacity was 400 pupils (200 per year group). In an average year, approximately 100 students continued into the sixth form from the lower school. Following the expansion of the lower school (Years 7 to 11), this number was expected to increase to 110 – a great place to be, as we had a committed audience (strong vertical integration) already. If we allowed our other secondary school pupils to apply for our sixth form as internals (our second secondary school had a phased growth, and therefore had a cohort of children who would soon be in the need of a sixth-form place), we could fill the majority of places (97.5 per cent) with Mossbournians, *ceteris paribus*. At the time, most of the sixth forms in the area were new, but there was a clear trend across the borough of pupils generally wanting to stay within the school that they knew, if possible.

Secondly, I needed to consider strategy as positioning: **How were we competing?** In considering the competitive advantage – if any – of different local schools-based sixth forms, I needed to break their 'product offer' down. The three areas that I selected were the subjects offered, the student outcomes and other factors. Collis and Rukstad (2008) provided a useful way in which to visualise Mossbourne's value proposition relative to its two biggest local competitors (see Figure 3).

- **Subject offer:** All three schools offer a broad range of subjects, with each school having a slight advantage over the other two in one of the three main subject categories.
- **Outcomes:** Mossbourne had a clear competitive advantage in outcomes across all three measures: average points per subject, AAB in at least two facilitating subjects and value added.
- **Other:** This includes other benefits of attending a specific sixth form that are not directly related to the curriculum offer, such as sports, drama clubs, debating, etc.

As you can see, the competitive advantages outlined are not valuable, scarce or costly for rivals to imitate, and therefore do not represent what Powell (2006, p. 9) would call a 'sustainable competitive advantage'. Whether a sustainable competitive advantage is achievable or desirable in state education is questionable. Collis and Rukstad (2008) and Powell (2006) offer but two ways in which to evaluate your strategic position; there are numerous other ways in which to analyse your strategic position, and one that I find particularly useful in education is PESTEL (political, economic, social, technological, environmental and legal – Oxford College of Marketing, n.d.). This whole process may seem extremely detailed, but looking before you leap is a wise man's game. The irony isn't lost on me, as my next chapter is about risk-taking, but when you are in a period of sustained improvement, you have time to breathe, time to think before you act and time to look before you leap.

After looking at the market, I moved on to look at the strategic prospects, i.e. our local competition, in more detail. One of our local competitors' strategic decisions to focus on creativity had provided it with a framework within which to make a number of critical decisions. Firstly, it had reduced its subject offer by eight, which would allow it to increase its average class size, a key fact in remaining viable in a reduced-funding environment. The sixth form had a clear strategy that ensured that it didn't cut any creative subjects, and as such it has maintained its value proposition as a creative hub. The school knew its mission

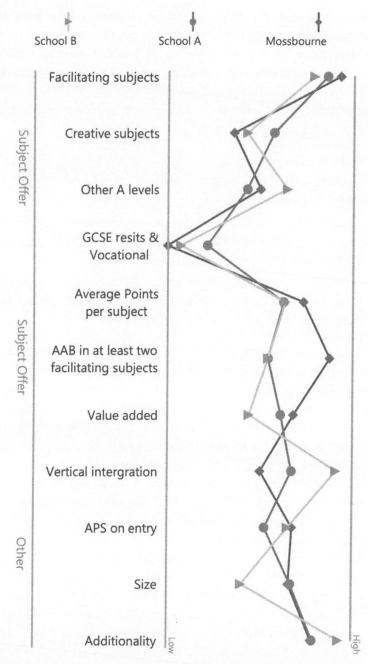

Figure 3 *Mossbourne's value proposition relative to its two biggest local competitors*

and stuck to it. As other sixth forms were reducing their subject offer to deal with funding cuts, this strategic approach turned out to be a significant advantage in the years that followed. Secondly, their focus on creativity allowed them to align their subject offers across their lower school and sixth form. This significantly reduced the number of subjects taught by a single teacher. Ensuring that all subjects were large enough to be taught by multiple teachers removed the possibility of a teacher becoming a unique resource and allowing the school to compete with what Frery et al. (2015, p. 71) would call 'ordinary resources'. This is an important competitive advantage in a climate of teacher shortages.

Mossbourne's focus on academic excellence appeared to be creating a self-perpetuating cycle of attracting the highest calibre of students, according to their GCSE grades, which in turn supported high outcomes and student acceptance at prestigious universities. However, the possible negative outcome of pursuing this strategy is that a single set of poor outcomes could result in a downward trajectory.

Our strategy quickly took shape. Leveraging our vertical scope worked. Not opening a second sixth form allowed us to use the spare building capacity creatively. We utilised this opportunity to increase the number of lower school pupils at our second school (MVPA), thus further enhancing our vertical integration. This put us in a unique position where we could fill up to 97.5 per cent of the 200 places internally. But in all this data, never forget the human factor; I learned this from creating the MAT central services infrastructure, and I wasn't going to make the same mistake twice. Children want to belong and feel a part of something. It was vitally important that students saw the one sixth form – the Mossbourne Sixth Form – as an extension of their school, no matter which one they attended from Year 7 to Year 11. Overall, our decision to vertically integrate places gave us a strong strategic position, but this would only work if the students, parents and staff believed that the one sixth form was their sixth form.

Having looked at our value proposition closely, I needed to decide on which trade-offs to make to distinguish ourselves from our competitors. Kim and Mauborgne (1997, p. 107) believe that a company should ask itself:

1. 'Which factors, that our industry takes for granted, should be eliminated?
2. Which factors should be reduced well below industry standard?
3. Which factors should be raised well above industry standard?
4. Which factors should be created that the industry has never offered?'

I asked these questions while paying careful attention to the impact on both financial and talent resources (teachers). There was no question that we needed to place our target of securing our students' places at 'prestigious universities' at the heart of all decisions, because the mission was always clear: to change children's lives for the better.

I made some tough decisions, but I made them from an informed position. The decisions that we make as leaders can have a generational impact on individuals and a community, particularly in education. I decided to move forward using Kim and Mauborgne's (1997) model, which focused on the concepts of eliminate, reduce, raise and never seen in order to create a new value curve (see Figure 4) for the sixth form.

- **Eliminate:** Traditionally, school-based sixth forms, especially in Hackney, had offered GCSE resits and vocational courses as a way of serving as many students as possible from their lower school. This was not always in the best interest of the student or the school. I took the decision to remove these options and focus purely on the A level subjects.

- **Reduce:** I looked to further reduce the subject offer in the creative and other A level subject categories to below industry standard. Only subjects that had a synergy with the lower school and minimum viable student numbers would be kept. The only exception would be subjects that were considered essential to maintaining Mossbourne's reputation as a high-performing organisation. Facilitating and traditional subject choices needed to be maintained, as they offered the greatest chance of acceptance to the top universities. For clarity, facilitating subjects are no longer preferred by Russell Group universities.

- **Raise:** We already had plans to raise vertical integration above the industry standard; however, if we maintained our current level of external applications, we had the potential to use the vertical integration to expand the sixth form and become the market leader by size. The raising of outcomes was fundamental to our success. By focusing on a niche subject market, improved outcomes followed.

- **Never seen:** We already offered several unique opportunities, including a rowing academy, but we needed to enhance the offer. It was clear that consideration should be given to other specialist programmes that were considered highly academic, as they would attract a higher calibre of students and teachers – for example, the creation of a specialist programme for aspiring medics or a specialist programme for students aspiring to Oxbridge.

The strategic benefits of these decisions were numerous. By having one sixth form and reducing the subject offer, we improved our financial position. We

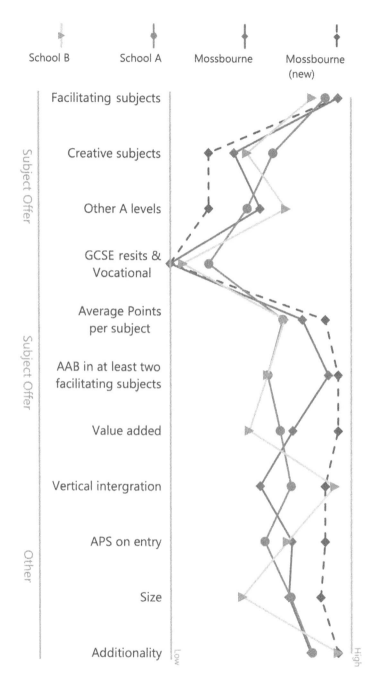

School B   School A   Mossbourne   Mossbourne (new)

Subject Offer

Facilitating subjects

Creative subjects

Other A levels

GCSE resits & Vocational

Subject Offer

Average Points per subject

AAB in at least two facilitating subjects

Value added

Other

Vertical intergration

APS on entry

Size

Additionality

Low   High

Figure 4 *Mossbourne's relative value proposition post-repositioning*

Doing what is right, not what is popular

were able to use the cost savings from the subject reductions to enhance the offer beyond the traditional curriculum.

The end result was a thriving sixth form with an exceptional offer beyond the curriculum. Each year, between five and ten per cent of our pupils gain acceptance to Oxbridge, with a further five per cent being accepted to medical school – not bad in a borough that had zero Oxbridge acceptances the year before the Mossbourne Sixth Form first opened its doors.

Research: The collecting of information about a particular subject

The Centre for Research in Social Policy at Loughborough University ranked Hackney as the third most deprived borough after housing costs (Stone, 2021) (see Figure 5). In Hackney, child poverty is a reality. Many of the pupils who attend my schools live in homes situated in deprived areas with high crime rates, low household incomes, unemployment and mental health issues. I feel that poverty has a huge impact on their experience of childhood. Schools are one institution (among others) that can play a key role in not allowing the statistical data and pupils' social backgrounds to become a barrier to success, by doing all that is possible to change the narrative.

In March 2016, poet Byron Vincent and university lecturer Anna Woodhouse hosted a show called *How to Turn Your Life Around* on BBC Radio 4. It referenced my

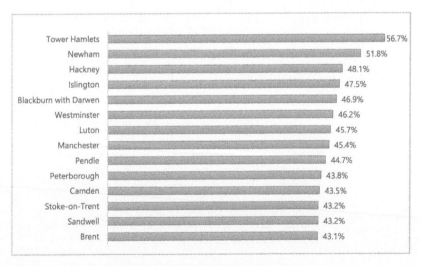

Figure 5 *Percentage of children in poverty after housing costs*

schools and resulted in a follow-up article by Woodhouse called 'How we learn to believe in ourselves'. The extract from the article below demonstrates why research is an important leadership skill, because it's a challenge to propel things forward without it. Being fuelled by curiosity means that you ask questions and immerse yourselves in discovering everything that there is to know about a topic. The deprivation indicators and other statistics found about Hackney offered a starting point for me to explore things, such as the use of passive supervision in school buildings and site design, but it is also a great catalyst for doing something never seen before. All children need safe environments in which to learn, live and flourish.

Woodhouse (2016) writes:

I think that most people have some experience at some stage in their school lives of being bullied. It was an intrinsic and inescapable part of the culture at the schools that I attended.

However, now there are schools that operate a strict 'zero-tolerance' approach. Opened in 2004, **Mossbourne, in Hackney,** *east London, was one of the first academy schools, and ranks in the top 1% of schools in the country for GCSE and A-level attainment. It has been judged 'outstanding' by Ofsted and described as 'amongst the very highest in the country'.*

What strikes you, walking around the school, is an almost eerie atmosphere of calm. I say eerie because, in my higher education (HE) outreach work, I go into a lot of schools, and I've never seen anything like Mossbourne. There is classroom after classroom of kids studiously, silently working.

The schools I work with are targeted because of their low progression rates into HE. Like these schools, Mossbourne serves what might otherwise be considered a disadvantaged catchment area. Yet it consistently boasts impressive progression rates. In 2011/12, 97% of Mossbourne's A-level students progressed to HE, and **30% secured places at Russell Group** *universities.*

The principal, Peter Hughes, says Mossbourne uses discipline to cultivate an alternative culture – of aspiration, rather than low expectation. I hardly consider myself a great disciplinarian, but the thing is it seems to work. And I'm passionate about raising aspirations, because I know from personal experience that low expectations can be paralysing.

Reproduced with permission from BBC News at **bbc.co.uk/news**

After making big choices regarding the sixth form, I wanted to spend time looking at enhancing the offer across our schools. This led to the creation of a foundation (www.mossbournecharity.org) to raise money specifically for providing students with additionality. The core focus of this fundraising is the five strands. After giving a robust argument as to why the move should be made to create one great sixth form, I used the research to further develop programmes that would have a monumental and significant impact on the lives of young people.

1. **The Rowing Academy:** A programme designed to provide students with the soft skills that come from competing at an elite level and one day change the face of British rowing.

2. **Medical bursary:** A programme designed to provide students with all the skills and experience necessary to attend medical, dentistry or veterinary school.

3. **Combined Cadet Force (CCF):** A programme designed to instil values in young people that will help them to get the most out of their lives and to contribute to their communities. It is not a fast-track to the army.

4. **The arts:** A programme designed to offer exposure to practices of creative expression, storytelling and cultural participation. At Mossbourne, all children must study 'the arts' until the end of Key Stage 4.

5. **Architecture and the built environment:** A programme for students who might be interested in careers in architecture, town planning, surveying or other careers in the built environment. Students work with some of the best architecture schools and practices in the country.

In addition to the five strands, we run Oxbridge prep, a programme of wider experiences and support with personal statements, interview and exam preparation, to ensure that our best and brightest maximise their Oxbridge application. The wider experience and university application support is provided to all students and not limited to students aspiring to go to Oxbridge – or even Russell Group universities, for that matter.

Creating progressive social change requires us to have both the data and the narrative. I know that we need to tell stories, and how important they are for young people from disadvantaged backgrounds, which is why I tell them throughout this book. If we want to bring about radical changes, it's important to use data to inform actions and to change the narrative. The strands are my small way of trying to do that.

'Do all the good you can,
By all the means you can,
In all the ways you can,
In all the places you can,

At all the times you can,
To all the people you can,
As long as ever you can.'
(Rule of life attributed to John Wesley)

Case Study – Stephen Hall, CEO Camden Learning, England

Introduction

I first met Stephen Hall when I was visiting one of his schools in London, Orchard Primary School, just before it was labelled 'outstanding'. I remember the visit like it was yesterday. I thought: 'If I ever run a primary school, I want it to be like this'. I've always felt that staff sending their child to your school is one of the best accolades a school can receive. I would send my child, if I had one, to any school that Stephen ran.

Stephen has held many roles since I have known him, including headteacher and executive headteacher, first of two schools, then of three. He has led three schools to 'outstanding' judgements in his career. Stephen is now focused on system change, first as Deputy Director of Education for Hackney Learning Trust and currently as CEO of Camden Learning. Stephen has always worked in local authority schools. He is testament to the fact that it isn't the type of school but the type of leader that counts.

Case study

Q. What advice would you give to someone going into a turnaround school?

A. I led four school turnarounds in my 12 years as a headteacher. Each was different, but there was a common thread: the sense of denial and self-protectionism in the leadership team and the school community. You have to push through that. To do this, you need to be clear about your vision and how you think the school should be. People don't always understand this until they see your vision in action.

Doing what is right, not what is popular

You need to spend the first six months highlighting the early wins so people can see the direction you're heading in. After around a year, you start to see proof of change, such as people speaking the language you want them to, taking their own initiative to actualise your vision and a general shift towards the direction you want the school to head in. It can be a rollercoaster. You may think you've taken a step forward, but then you take two steps back.

Q. Do you have some examples of when you have had to make right but unpopular decisions?

A. The first school I took on was a small local authority primary school in special measures. Sadly, it was the governors who were most in denial about the poor education being provided at the school. The results were in the bottom one per cent of London schools, but they couldn't accept that their school was failing children. To get them to buy into my vision, I had to be honest and clear with them about why I was doing what I was doing; always relating it back to the children. In any situation like this, it's important to have a leader. As the headteacher, that leader is you. You have to stick your neck out and stand by what you believe in. I put forward to the governors: 'This is what we're going to do and why, and these are my measurables. In six months' time, you can check on progress, but we can't stay as we are now'. This meant there was a steer for discussion in governors' meetings. You must be brave and clear about what you want!

Another example of when you need to take a stand on something that people may not like is when it comes to popular members of staff. Other teachers and parents may not recognise a popular staff member's failings because they like them and can't see that they're stuck in a rut with their professional output. The way to navigate this is to allow people to have their dignity. Ultimately, it's a job and they're committed, but they're sometimes committed in the wrong ways.

The most dramatic example I have of this is from another local authority school that needed rapid change. It was very clear that the headteacher was the problem. There were low expectations throughout the school and there was some shocking teaching going on, but the headteacher was very popular with staff, even when the school was self-evaluating as 'inadequate'. When he left, a lot of staff left with him but this was ultimately a good thing as he'd poisoned the well before I arrived by setting me up as the enemy, conflating me with Ofsted. It would have been very hard for me to get those teachers to buy into my vision. No one wants half the staff leaving, but if that's what needs to happen for the school to move forwards, then that's what has to happen. It's that saying, 'if you want to make an omelette, you have to break a few eggs'.

That particular school is now 'outstanding', and it has sustained that exceptional quality for some time. Initially, I had to fill the vacancies as quickly as possible, but then I looked at a longer-term recruitment strategy for great teachers who could sustain my vision for how the school should look. If you have to change the culture in a school, you have to change the mindset first. You may need to be honest with people – if they haven't bought into the new direction, they can leave.

Q. That all sounds very challenging. How do you stay focused and on point?

A. It can be a difficult and lonely place to be in while you're implementing changes and having so many difficult conversations. The thing that underpins it, though, is the idea of what's right for the pupils. When you walk around the school and see what's going on in the classroom, you know which classes are good and which ones aren't. It gives you an overriding ambition to get all the classes to be as good as the best ones! That never goes away, even when you have an 'outstanding' school. The leaders at those schools are constantly seeking out ways that they can improve. That sense of restlessness is what makes a great school leader.

Q. You have talked about moving on teachers and leaders who don't meet your standards. What do you do with the 'maverick' who is a great teacher but doesn't buy in 100%?

A. You may have a teacher who is good, they go the extra mile, the parents love them, but you know that long term, they don't belong in the school – the 'maverick'.

The 'maverick' is another example of a time you need to have a vital and difficult conversation. When you're dealing with this situation, you have to first get to know the culture and community of the school. Who are the key governors, parents and people who need that extra airtime?

In the first few weeks you will make mistakes, but you learn from those and adapt to the existing culture. It's important to celebrate things that are important to that school. The 'maverick' fits into this in a sense. In the beginning, if they are doing a good job and the children are safe, you embrace them as part of that school's culture. If you intend to keep them, you can acknowledge their status and accept that they won't do everything in the exact way you want them to, but give them some flexibility while you're getting organised. The tipping point comes when there's a body of staff who have embraced the new culture and you can see this through the way they communicate with pupils and parents. There's a different level of professionalism in the way they go about their business. The way they conduct themselves is healthy and warm but still professional. It's at this point that the 'maverick' starts to look less great because the sea has risen, and they haven't risen with it. That's when you need to have the difficult conversation. But you do it with dignity, and you are clear about why you're doing it. Be prepared for them to be unhappy but know that you're doing it for the greater good of the school.

Even in the healthiest of settings there are going to be some people who are unhappy. I think moving unhappy people on is difficult, but you're creating a whole-school culture, and if adults are getting in the way of creating that, then it's not such a hard decision. They might be doing an OK job in the classroom, but the impact of their negativity outside of it has an impact on the school's overall culture.

Q. You have had to make some big decisions in the interests of children. Have you ever got it wrong?

A. I've had lots of successes but being humbled is also an important part of leadership. I have learned to listen more, seek other opinions and admit when I am wrong. There have been many times when I've made mistakes and I've had to learn from them, usually when I have not taken enough account of the context or given something enough time. I once implemented a school management information system (MIS) without appreciating its impact on wider systems. Other examples are recruiting poorly and having to quickly act to put things right, and not picking up on parents or staff who needed that extra bit of time. I once moved on a teacher who had lots of potential, but I didn't allow enough time to develop them. The school was in a highly pressured situation but I made the call too quickly. It's one of those things that haunt me because I know it wasn't the right decision. I only hope that they are still teaching now.

Q. Is there anything you would tell a leader who is striving for the best to watch out for?

A. Be mindful of the culture you're creating and how this can seed more negative elements. The culture in one school I led as an executive headteacher went awry, and I had responsibility for that. There was an overemphasis on results and outcomes, and of course those are important, but not at all costs and at unrealistic levels. I hadn't realised how far the culture at the school had slipped in the wrong direction. It was a sudden and humble realisation for me to see how bad things had become under my watch. Reflecting on school culture and its wider impact has made me a better leader. My hubris is more measured, and I'm alert to exactly what we're measuring.

Q. Any final words?

A. Always bring it back to the children. That is why we are here as teachers and school leaders. It's surprising how this sometimes gets forgotten and the focus ends up on adults. The young people are always the most fun, meaningful and inspiring aspect of the job.

The solution

Anything is possible; the only limitation is you. Let me explain. It's a given that people are generally afraid of getting into trouble. Generally, we all want to get things right and follow the straight path. There is a fear that if you don't do X, something bad will happen, and there is some substance to this fear; however, if you never try something new, nothing changes or evolves.

We are bombarded with what we should do, but no one asks: 'What will happen if I don't?' Well, very few people do. We often don't even know who 'they' are – the people asking the questions of us, like some omnipotent Wizard of Oz-like figure. Are they the DfE? The local authority? Who knows? Therefore, it's important to ask yourself these questions to challenge your perceptions and decision-making:

- Who is telling me?
- What happens if I don't?

If you keep asking yourself these two questions, you may start to realise that the illusive 'they' blocking the idea is actually you. Schools can transform the way in which children see themselves in the world, and help to turn aspirations into tangible opportunities and outcomes. What separates out the very best schools is the level of belief that they have for every one of their pupils – starting from nowhere, with just an idea.

As an example, we built a very successful rowing team in the heart of Hackney. In 2022, the Year 10 boys' team from our Rowing Academy celebrated finishing second in the National Schools Regatta (Woolcock, 2022). As teachers, we need to think of our pupils' education from a 'whole child' perspective. That isn't taking away from the importance of academic outcomes, but rather pushing our children to achieve their full potential in every area of their life. We want our children to know that nothing is impossible. Showing the country that a team of pupils from an inner-city London school (who typically wouldn't have an opportunity to get into a sport such as rowing) could excel and finish second in the largest rowing regatta for juniors in Great Britain is proof of this belief. This step was just the beginning. The wider impact is still causing ripple effects. There is a lack of diversity in sports such as rowing – fewer than five per cent of British rowers identify as being from a Black, Asian or a minority ethnic group. The Mossbourne rowing team is made up of around 40 per cent of pupils who identify as being from this group. We always show our children that the sky is not the limit for them, and that they can achieve anything that they put their minds to. If we want our kids to dream big, we should make sure that we dream big for them too.

The final words

When Mossbourne began, and the declarations were made about what the school was planning to achieve, people didn't believe that it would be possible. It puzzles me that there are those that want schools to fail children, especially those with a challenging start to life. The naysayers were opposed to the aspirational goals and claims of Mossbourne to such an extent that when we did achieve the impossible, accusations of cheating were flung about like mud. Efforts were made to try to discredit and question the validity of the achievements that the school had made.

I think that the BBC article by Anna Woodhouse (2016) helps to summarise this chapter in ways that will resonate with many. Woodhouse states as an opener to her piece that one of the central challenges that society faces is how to improve opportunities for those who have had a difficult start. My final word: many leaders make excuses as to why they do not achieve their goals; don't be one of them.

Top tips

- Know when to take time to analyse a problem in detail.
- Know what your non-negotiables are.
- Do the research. Find new avenues and enriching opportunities for your students so that they can dream big with your help.

4 Taking risks

Political decisions and initiatives in education come and go, but we need to stay steady. Knowing what changes to make, prioritising the quality of teaching and focusing on outcomes and achievements for children are the core jobs for a leader. It takes confidence in oneself and the organisation's mission and vision to follow through with this. Having confidence in your provision and what it delivers is fundamental. This chapter looks at the role of risk-taking through the leadership skills of scrutiny and background, with a particular focus on minimising rather than removing risk. I'll tell you about some of my least proud moments, namely Umbrellagate, and introduce you to Katie Bedborough, a remarkable woman whom I met on my MBA and from whom I have learned so much, in this chapter's case study. My final thoughts look at the benefit and result of blending qualitative and quantitative data.

The yarn

I finished school in Young, a small country town in Australia, and after university and a year teaching in the gateway to the outback (Bourke) I went back there to teach. Three years in – now 25 years old – I found myself at the point in my life where I was thinking about buying a block of land and building a house – a very common thing in rural Australia. I found my block of land, went to the bank for a loan and waited. The bank made an error. Instead of sending me the deposit – ten per cent of the purchase price – they sent me a cheque for the full amount. I looked at this huge cheque for a very long time. Thoughts of home ownership, settling down in the town in which I finished school and teaching at the local school for the next few decades flashed in and out of my mind. I asked myself a life-changing question: Is this the rest of my life? Nothing more, nothing less – just that simple question, which caused a monumental ripple effect in my life.

I decided that day that I was going to travel. I tore up the cheque from the bank and I sold everything that could be sold (this included my Honda VTR 1000 motorbike, which I loved), put a few things in storage and gave everything else away. I used some of the money from the items I'd sold and bought a standby, one-way ticket to London, said my goodbyes and travelled to Sydney. I had four days left before the flight to get some sort of plan together, and this is when

I saw the agency ad in the *Sydney Morning Herald* for supply teaching in London. I gave them a call; they asked me to come in and I did my interview that day. They handed me my paperwork (they knew that I would beat the postman to England) and the address of their office in London. With my paperwork in my backpack, they sent me on my way. I jumped on a plane and was off.

It's worth knowing that I had never left Australia before this, and had only been on a plane with an engine once in my life, when going on an internal trip to Queensland. I had been really into flying gliders (in case the engine comment threw you earlier) following winning a scholarship, but that's a story for another time and place. When I boarded the plane to London, I still had no concrete accommodation, as I hadn't had time to sort anything long term, but the agency gave me the address of a hostel where I could stay (I was hoping that they had a bed when I arrived) until I found my feet. I'm aware that this sounds risky and that most people reading this could not imagine doing something similar. However, the point to this yarn is this. I put two specific things in place. The first was that I did my research, albeit very quickly. In the New South Wales (NSW) education system, you could: a) leave your job for a 12-month sabbatical and still return to the same school, or b) leave for a 24-month sabbatical and be placed in a school in NSW upon your return. Amazing, right? The second safety net I put in place was to make sure that I had a credit card with a limit high enough to get me a flight back home.

In our schools, we put safeguards in place all the time; leaders regularly forward-plan for many different scenarios. The lesson here is that something might look risky on the outside but underneath there may have been considerable energy given to risk analysis and in-depth thinking that took place prior to it happening. You can't be exceptional if you walk a path that avoids risks at all costs. In business, we talk about a risk–benefit analysis. What are the benefits of doing X? What is the worst possible outcome? How can I mitigate the risks? In education, we often try to nullify the risk instead of mitigating it. Remember the term 'risk–benefit analysis', as it opens up a wealth of possibilities.

I like to visualise my risk–benefit analysis on a simple two-dimensional plane (see Figure 6). Obviously, it would be great if every new idea or initiative was in the top right, but they rarely are. Therefore, I ask the following questions:

- Is the possible benefit significant?
- How can I move the risk to the right, from unacceptable to acceptable or even to minimal?

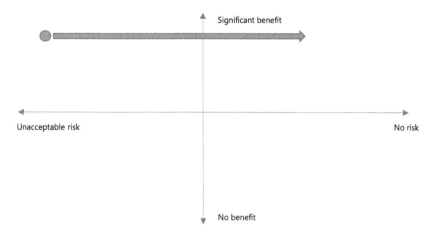

Figure 6 *Risk-benefit analysis*

In my travelling example, the benefit of seeing the world is a significant one. I was able to move the risk from unacceptable to acceptable by taking a sabbatical and ensuring that I had a credit card. I didn't nullify the risk. If it all crashed and burned, I would end up back home without any possessions and the debt of a London-to-Sydney plane ticket, but I would at least have a job. Taking risks means that you will, of course, make mistakes at times, but it's important to see these as opportunities for growth. This raises the bar for yourself and others. Would I be the same person that I am now if I'd kept the loan cheque and built a house in my hometown to live in? I'll never know but I think that it's highly unlikely, and I'm happy that I took the leap.

Leadership skills

Scrutiny: Critical observation or examination

The school was in the top one per cent and I was preparing to build a new secondary school. The English Baccalaureate had not long been introduced. Life without levels was here and GCSE exams were in the middle of being reformed. Education was in a state of flux – the perfect time to become a principal. The school had been built on the high-stakes accountability model and had been very successful. With the exam system in flux, governors breathing down my neck (as a new principal) and the new Chief Inspector rewriting the standards, it was the perfect time to change the way that we monitored and developed teaching and learning. Or was it?

As an old-school advanced skills teacher (ASTs were employed in roles that included an element of work dedicated to supporting and improving the practice of teaching colleagues in their own schools and other schools in the area), I had significant experience of developing the practices of teachers across the spectrum, from early career teachers (ECTs) to established teachers, in my own and other schools. From my own professional development as a teacher, I can recall only one or two moments where a formal observation had provided useful feedback that had resulted in a positive change in my practice. In fact, there were even times where I taught my formal observation lesson to another class as practice first, before teaching it in the formal observation. Why would anyone teach a lesson twice? The answer is simple. Under a high-stakes accountability system, I would do everything in my power to ensure that each of my formal observations were as close to perfect as possible. This included practising and improving them. This was the pressure cooker in which most teachers at the time found themselves (and some still do now). At the time, my school was no different.

We had three formal observations a year. In addition, there would be two or three external visitors who would grade your lessons as part of a practice inspection or external validations of the school. And watch out if you got a low grade. Those of us who have been in education for some time have all seen the impact that this structure has on colleagues or themselves. We've all seen the teacher who never marked their books, never met deadlines and never planned structured lessons pulling an outstanding-graded lesson out the bag because they knew how to meet all the points on the observation checklist. They would keep the observer entertained and enthralled throughout the 45-minute lesson (performance).

Knowing what I knew from my own personal teaching experiences, from Doug Lemov's teaching and learning toolkit (Teach like a Champion) and from the role of marginal gains in David Brailsford's Team Sky success (Clear, n.d.), it felt right that we should move from a stressful, high-stakes, low-frequency monitoring model to a low-stakes, high-frequency developmental model. (High frequency means every three to four weeks, or maybe more for a teacher who is struggling or who wants to work on a specific area of their practice; all ECTs in England now have this model of instructional coaching.) Brailsford, the performance director of the British cycling team, focused on marginal gains when he was appointed in 2003. His focus and success were a big influence on my model for teaching and learning. He set about making small improvements for the team across a range of areas that would have a far-reaching impact. This approach propelled the British cycling team into the forefront of the sport globally, after decades of defeats. It was also behind Team Sky's Tour de France victories.

When I think back, it seems obvious. We had been approaching children's learning using low-stakes, high-frequency, incremental teaching, learning and feedback for years. Yet teachers couldn't see the wood for the trees due to the red tape and scrutiny. Why did we think that the way in which we teach adults should be any different to how we teach children? Is there a magic switch that is flipped at 18 years old that changes the complete make-up of our brain and how we learn?

Risk–benefit analysis

If we are already in the top one per cent, why change the model? What is the benefit? The risk is obvious: change. But sometimes you need to look at things more deeply. The school had a hand-picked, exceptional selection of staff from its inception. This included approximately ten ASTs (to offer a reference point, my previous secondary school had zero when I arrived and two when I left). A large budget, as one of the first academies in the country, meant that there were basically no restrictions to the available resources. A phased beginning meant that the school started with one cohort and proceeded to increase in size, one year group at a time. Along with all the other academies at this time, the school was given all the ingredients needed for success.

Different types of leadership are needed throughout a school's journey. Start-ups and schools graded 'inadequate' that are being moved to 'requires improvement' and 'good' all need a different type of leader and leadership to achieve success. Ignore this at your peril. When I became the principal, the school was no longer a start-up; it was a maturing organisation. The systems now needed to evolve to match this new phase of the academy's life. The school was slowly losing the amazing, highly talented, evangelical teachers who had been in place from the start and who knew instinctively how everything worked. The landscape was changing and if you don't move forwards, you go backwards. We found ourselves struggling to find the quality of staff (has anything changed?). We needed to maintain the environment where learning was the norm and children achieved great outcomes. Therefore, doing nothing represented a low-benefit, medium-risk scenario. Ultimately, we may have ended up in a situation where we didn't have the teachers with the skills required to maintain excellence. I could have easily become the David Moyes of education.

What to do?

I decided to provide teachers with high-quality, incremental feedback (like our students) in order to improve their practice and move their typicality forward. If every lesson was good or better, every day, then my students would be receiving an outstanding education. I believed that if we improved the way in which we gave teachers feedback and gave them time back, then we could not just maintain but actually improve pupil outcomes.

What did I want in practice?

1. Remove the cycle of three formal observations a year.

2. Introduce unannounced drop-ins within a developmental framework.

3. Leaders to undertake a minimum of one observation (feedback session) per week.

4. No judgement of lesson (evaluate elements of lessons instead).

5. No teachers to plan or prepare for an observation. Teachers to focus on planning and delivery of lessons.

6. Introduce a backbone of expectations for feedback:

    a. Every teacher to know what they are good at, what they are working on and what feedback has been given.

    b. Every observer to know what the teacher is working on, what they are good at and what other observers have said, so that they can build upon the previous feedback. No teacher to be given contradictory feedback.

    c. Every leader to have the class's information (pupil context, attainment and progress data) to hand while observing.

    d. Staff falling below the expected standard in an element of teaching practice to be revisited within a week and supported to improve, if required.

7. Every leader to have access to the feedback for the teachers for whom they are responsible, so that they can plan CPD at key stage, department and whole-school levels.

8. SLT to receive weekly information about the quality of teaching and learning across the school from feedback data collected, and not anecdotal heuristics.

Removing all formal observations and replacing them with drop-ins (which included feedback) didn't happen overnight. I had to think about ways in which to mitigate the risks and bring people on board; I was a new principal and, in the eyes of many staff members, I hadn't earned my stripes yet. You might wonder what the risk is of removing all formal observations and switching to a developmental model. Surely there are no risks in dumping formal observations and replacing them with regular, low-stakes drop-ins?

Here I was, talking about new research, drops-ins, transparency and moving to a developmental model, full of coaching and mentoring across a whole school, to the masses. It was a huge risk. I was talking a different language. People need to be approached in ways that suit their personalities to get the best out of them (we will explore this further when we look at archetypes in the next chapter). We needed to change with the times, and I needed a road map to implement the change. I started by listing the key risks and the associated issues that would need to be mitigated if we were to be successful.

Key risks	Issue to be mitigated
More than three observations per year	Union mandate was for a maximum of three observations per year
Unannounced drop-ins	Union mandate was for all observations to be announced, citing teacher stress
Removal of formal observations	Without formal observation, how would standards be maintained?
Quality of feedback	More people doing more feedback created more room for poor-quality feedback
No lesson judgements	How does one analyse the quality of the provision?

I needed my champions. I needed to iron out any issues on a small scale before we went global (school-wide launch). I trialled the model with new department leaders who understood developmental coaching, were keen and wanted to drive this forward. The idea was to build from the middle out, rather than from the top down. I sweetened the deal by giving all the leaders tablets with which to conduct the observations. I knew that the unannounced part had the potential to unnerve people and kill the initiative before it started. To avoid the blow-back, I explained how it would reduce workload and how we were looking for typicality, and not one-off perfection. Therefore, no single drop-in would ever be used to decide the quality of anyone's teaching. The aim was to build a picture of typicality over time to improve teachers' practice. The reduction of workload happened because there was now no need to write reports or collate the observations; this would be done by the software. There was also no longer a need for observation prep by the teacher.

I needed a way in which to capture all this developmental information in a single place. We needed to aggregate the qualitative and quantitative data from the drop-ins in order to accurately assess the quality of teaching and learning across all departments and the school as a whole. This is where I came up with the idea of ProgressTeaching and developed a platform where all of this information could be stored. I mitigated the risk of moving from a high-stakes to a low-stakes model by designing a platform that offered transparency and gathered all the information in one place. All teachers and leaders could see the observations, with appropriate restrictions of course. For the first time, the leaders were making informed decisions based on all the feedback given to teachers in real time. No more out-of-date information from the last observation cycle. No more sweeping judgements based on heuristics.

Background: The circumstances or situation prevailing at a particular time or underlying a particular event

In their book *Great by Choice* (2011), Jim Collins and Morten T. Hansen talk about the concept of firing bullets and then cannonballs. The bullets represent low-cost, low-risk and low-distraction items. Cannonballs represent the much larger risks. I present to you: Umbrellagate. This was not my proudest moment.

Hackney was and still is known for gang violence, and it continues to be no secret that many of my pupils, to this day, have a gang affiliation. For some, it is impossible to avoid and their main hope is to survive their childhood. They all know now to leave gang-fuelled animosity at the school gate before they come onto school premises. They also now know that any criminal activity committed in school uniform will warrant a sanction. Please note here that I believe that any child, even a so-called perpetrator of crime, is a victim. Legislation within England is slowly catching up with this view, particularly within national safeguarding documentation around county lines (see The Children's Society, n.d.) to stop the criminalisation of children. This hard line regarding expectations of behaviour has enabled the children who come to our schools to be children. I see them play (yes, in my secondary schools as well), support each other and bring their authentic, unjudged self to school as a result. This is a beautiful sight to see, especially because I have seen and know the challenges that they face outside the Mossbourne Federation bubble.

However, to get to this stage, there was some trial and error. The story that follows – Umbrellagate – will go down in Mossbourne folk law. Winter was coming. England in winter is cold and wet and horrid. Most people wrap up as though ready to start an expedition to the Arctic, which also requires a hood (but only when it is raining if you are a Mossbournian). The children started to walk the cold, wintery streets of Hackney on the way to school, with hoods up, hats pulled down and scarfs wrapped around their necks. In this period of history, hoods and hoodies had extremely negative connotations for young people – unjust, but the stereotype was there, and it gave a loose excuse for stop-and-search and imposed judgements. We didn't want any of my children being stopped for simply walking to school. There was also the reality that young people did use hoodies to disguise themselves when they were engaging in negative activities.

So, we bought umbrellas. Lots and lots of umbrellas. And we insisted that pupils didn't wear hoods. Now we were not saying that wearing a hood meant that you were in a gang or partaking in criminal activity, but I had previously worked in other London schools where this was the case, and adults and children were not safe. We wrote letters to parents and carers, bought all children a bog-standard black umbrella, gave them all out, set the expectation and waited. True to form, the British weather didn't disappoint. The rain did arrive, as did the wind, a fierce, unforgiving, blustering wind. Children were parachuted around the streets of Hackney, umbrellas were turned inside out, broken and left discarded, dancing in the wind, lying snapped in the street and rolling into the roads. It was carnage.

We learned that umbrellas are not effective. We failed fast, learned fast and improved fast. We understood that there are reasons why children – and adults, for that matter – wear hoods. They are simple and effective and they work. We could see that we were attempting to fight against the tide by swimming without water. It made no sense. We abandoned the umbrellas and told the children that they could wear hoods (but only when it was raining – we were Mossbourne, after all) and they have worn them ever since.

Case study: Katie Bedborough, ACMA, MBA, CFO at technology company, England

Introduction

I first met Katie while doing my Executive MBA at Oxford. I thought that my path to Oxford was interesting until Katie told that she got an E and two Ns in her A levels. They clearly weren't a reflection of her ability. As we chatted more, Katie's story of climbing through the ranks got ever more interesting. She wasn't someone that was going to allow social convention to dictate her life. It was like her whole life was constructed around a risk–benefit analysis. Who better to contribute to this chapter about risk than Katie?

Case study

Q. You've always taken big risks. It seems like you have a very 'go for it and find out later' attitude.

A. I think that if you have common sense, you can do anything you put your mind to. I remember reading an article that said that women only apply for jobs if they meet 100 per cent of the criteria, whereas men apply for a job if they only meet 60 per cent of the criteria. I decided that I wasn't going to do less than men did – if I met 60 per cent of the criteria, I was going to go for it. I would take a risk and bet on myself being able to learn whatever was needed. I have a learning mindset and when I look back over the last ten years at how far I've come and how much I've learnt, I know that in another ten years I'll know so much more than I do now.

Q. Has your appetite for risk changed over time, with new positions and changes in responsibility?

A. I don't take big risks like I used to. Now that I'm a mum, and a solo one at that, it's not just me that I need to think about. I was recently offered an opportunity to work at another start-up. I know the CEO really well. This is the sort of opportunity that I would have jumped at in the past – working with an almost all female leadership team in a deep tech company (almost unheard of!), but I found myself very nervous about going to another Oxford University spin-out company because I remember how nerve-racking it can get working for a company that isn't fully established and making a profit.

I have to think about my mortgage and nursery bills now. I burned through my savings in taking a year of maternity leave, and so I don't have the safety net to go to another job where I could lose my job suddenly. The downside if it didn't work out was that I might not be able to get another job quick enough to provide for my son. He's my priority now. He's my responsibility and I can't take risks like I used to.

Q. That's something that I can completely understand. In the education space, I have to manage risks in a certain way because I'm dealing with children's lives. You're dealing with your son's life and you've got to take a very different approach to risks.

A. I have fundamentally shifted the way I think. It's all about risk mitigation now. When you're dealing with a human being, not just a piece of software, you have to think differently. If I look at my life so far, taking the risks that I have has massively elevated what I've achieved. I've done so much more than I ever could have imagined. I wouldn't change the risks that I've taken. I'm much keener to have safety nets now, though, whereas before I would jump headfirst into something without them. Perhaps if I still had my savings I'd have been more comfortable thinking about that job!

I think if you're risking just yourself, it's much easier to take a chance than if you're risking someone else. It's a bigger and more difficult decision that you have to make. I have to know that if I take a risk and it doesn't work out, I'm not going to make my child homeless. Before my boy arrived, I would have just been able to sell my house and either rent a small flat or move back with my folks!

Q. If you were to give people top tips on risk analysis, what would they be?

A. Don't always focus on the worst-case scenario. You need to scenario-plan but the chances of the worst-case scenario happening are really slim. People tend to spend all their time focused on Armageddon, which is around a one in a million chance of happening. They forget about the mid-range risks with a high probability.

Typically, I use a risk matrix that focuses on likelihood and impact. I score each of those factors on a scale of one to four and multiply the result.

Then I focus on the highest scoring items (nine and above), i.e. the risks that have a three or four score for both likelihood and impact. These are the risks for which you need to create a mitigation strategy.

Q. In education, people often try to avoid risk. In the private sector you assess risk and decide whether it's worth taking the gamble. For example, with HR issues you need to think about the likeliness that somebody will take you to a tribunal, how much money they're costing you, how you can move them out of the business in a sensible way, etc. When you apply that to a school, you have to think that it is children's lives that this person is ruining. A bad teacher affects 150 children a day.

A. Risk is unavoidable. You will always encounter an element of risk in your day. You take a risk by walking out of your front door. The best people assess and do what they can to mitigate. You can't ever remove risk, but you can reduce the impact or likelihood to a level with which you are comfortable.

Avoiding risk also avoids benefit. Take my example of the job offer – I am saying no to this opportunity, but in ten years the company could be as big as Google and I will have missed the opportunity to be living in a mansion and never worrying about providing for my son again! It's about finding a balance, because you want those opportunities but with a downside that you are comfortable encountering should the worst happen.

The solution

Something easily said but not easily achieved is creating a culture where calculated risks are encouraged. Risk-taking is among the qualities found in exemplary leaders as identified by Gardner and Laskin (2011), who write: 'The capacity to take risks speaks to a confidence that one will at least sometimes attain success' (p. 33). Leaders must also accept the fact that they might fail. This explains why many principals are possibly reluctant to take risks. They are accountable to so many stakeholders who do not readily accept failure.

It's critical not just to acknowledge when things go right but also to create a culture where people try ideas and where experiments are congratulated, whether they are successful or not. If you don't celebrate calculated risk, you will create a risk-averse culture. Only celebrating risk when people are successful doesn't engender a culture of continuous improvement. This can be painful, especially when you are dealing with children's futures, but that's why we talk about measured risks. Remember to praise the individual, their thoughtfulness and the mitigations that they put in place, whether it worked or not.

This is the method mirrored in many places but most notably in the world of Formula 1 (which is the embodiment of high-stakes accountability), where they undertake a retrospective, whether they win or lose. In educational terms, you may do an annual case study on Key Stage 2 SATs (standard assessment tests) data, no matter what the outcomes; have a retrospective on department performance when there has been a major success, in order to look at the lessons learned in detail; or scrutinise the observations of ECTs across your school to look at trends that can inform CPD. Whether you win or lose, whether outcomes are great or bad, undertaking a retrospective to answer these three questions is just great practice as a leader.

What do we keep doing?

What can we start doing?

What can we stop doing?

The final words

Although I'm not a believer in grading schools or lessons, I do believe that you can evaluate parts of the whole and that this is the most effective way in which to bring about positive change, whether that be in teacher practice, the curriculum or pupil outcomes. As a mathematician and a leader, I'm aware that you can either have qualitative information, collected using questionnaires, interviews, observations or feedback, or quantitative information. Is one type of data better than the other? I believe that the best approach is to blend the two, especially in education, where so many things can't be captured by a single number. The numbers often provide the big picture and point you in a direction, but it is often only by looking at the underlying narrative that the true picture is revealed. Teachers and children are more than a number.

High-performing schools are ones that promote continuous growth, nurture development and encourage leaders to take measured risks. They ensure that children and their learning is at the forefront of every discussion and strategic decision. Be afraid, but do it anyway; just make sure that you analyse the risk first. Don't be risk-averse, or you may never be an exceptional leader. There is a lot of noise that can easily distract leaders from their core role and mission, and my role as CEO in my trust is to keep people on the right path by ensuring that my principals and senior leaders can focus on the core business of teaching and learning. Keep working towards the goals that you want for your schools and your children, but never, ever believe that an umbrella can solve a problem.

Top tips

- Risk is an essential part of success. Mitigate it but don't try to nullify it.
- Risk management is a balancing act, as mitigation often dulls the benefit.
- Celebrate measured risk, even when something fails.
- Undertake retrospectives, especially when you succeed.

A small but mighty baby elephant

Shhhhhh, they are sleeping. It's been a full-on morning in the nursery; the small world tuff trays are full of glitter and shaving foam.

Throughout my years in leadership, I have developed the utmost admiration for primary schools and the work that takes place in them. As you know, I never anticipated that I would be the CEO of an all-through MAT, yet here I am. I feel that I am ever the better leader for it. Yes, leaderships skills are transferable – I discuss this throughout the book – but I wanted to ensure that we all recognise that this portability of skills also applies to phases in the education system. Although I am a secondary maths teacher at my core, the structure of my teaching degree in Oz had elements with a heavy weighting in child psychology – a serendipitous gift. A gift that has ensured that I nurture this elephant, have high aspirations for it and never underestimate it. All this being said, I've also confessed to the stupidity of my youth and my undertaking in my first few years of headship of several monumental tasks. Two of these were taking on a turn-around primary and building a new one.

The first primary was in a dire state when I went to visit it with a member of the local authority during the spring term. I remember walking into a Year 2 classroom where the carpet had worn away so badly that you could see through to the floor underneath. The six-year-olds were sitting on concrete floors. It had already been rebranded under a previous government's fresh start initiative. It had never in its history been graded as good. I left that visit knowing that I had to take the school on and bring it into the federation.

Although teaching and learning is teaching and learning, I underestimated the importance of understanding the primary sector when turning the school around. I had a limited network that reached into these spaces for teaching and learning. This meant that I had few resources, no curriculum and no teachers to parachute in. Tasks like refurbishing the building, bringing in IT (information technology) infrastructure and implementing an effective finance system were straightforward, but the systems for a primary curriculum intent and implementation needed to be created from scratch. Turning this school around took a village – an absolute community of focused individuals – after a prolonged period of laying foundations and several false dawns:

- children achieving outcomes in line with the national average (only for them to hit rock bottom a year later)
- leadership and management being graded 'good' by Ofsted (only to be downgraded later).

The tipping point came when we finally had the right people doing the right jobs at the right time. None of you will be surprised that the right leadership was fundamental to this, but another key factor was the fact that the leaders facilitated the two primary schools working together and sharing good practice. What I've always known and what this drove home is that it is possible to have an exceptional secondary school that can stand alone due to the monumental capacity that it has. However, the primary sector needs and wants to work together as a community.

When we achieved the 'good' grade, which the community and children deserved and had worked extremely hard for, the village celebrated. **The school had never been graded 'good' in the 30-odd years of Ofsted's existence. I'll say it again for the people at the back. The school now provides a good education.** As I've said before, as much as we need to reform Ofsted, we do want the external validation. We want to know as educators and we want the community to know that we are providing a 'good' education for the children whom we have been entrusted to educate. What it did give us was the confirmation that we were changing children's lives for the better through creating environments where learning is the norm.

Our start-up primary is a very different story. Very much like MVPA, we were able to work with the council and the architects to design the building. Again, I was in a room with builders and architects looking at blueprints, and déjà vu struck when they started highlighting the red tape issues. 'You can't build here because HS1 runs under the site.' 'You can't build here because the water mains for East London run through here.' 'You must give Thames Water access to the ground here, here and here at any time they want.' I'm pleased to say that, despite all of the challenges, the architects were able to design another award-winning building for us. It is also officially part of the London 2012 Olympics legacy. Remember – I still needed the right people doing the right jobs, so I looked for my primary school equivalent of Veronica Carol. I found them thanks to Glen (whom you will meet later). Among the contributions that they made to the building were:

- the positioning of the toilets in Early Years to support continuous provision
- numerous break-out rooms (now that the school is full, we still don't have enough)
- secure tea and coffee points on every floor, because no one ever has time enough to make a hot drink.

And of course, we implemented passive supervision, among the other things that we'd learned. This was our third new building after all.

I knew very early on that the building was never going to be ready on time. So we had to start the school with less than 30 reception children, who were picked up by our minibus and deposited at our turn-around school in the repurposed nursery (turned reception class). We were also established now and able to hit the ground running, as all support structures were in place. Through using our knowledge of start-ups and the leadership and staff body's knowledge of primary, we were able to achieve 'outstanding' in our first inspection (the second year in our new building).

If you are really going to make a difference to a child's life, you can do a lot more when you start from the age of three than you can when they start in Year 7. That is why children who attend a federation primary school get priority access to a federation secondary school, and ultimately into the sixth form. There is no point being an all-through MAT if you keep the phases separated. If you are going to have primary and secondary schools, you need to figure out what the curriculum is from EYFS to the sixth form. The biggest challenge is unpicking what everyone can be learning from each other without it being tokenistic or resorting to the classic 'The secondary experts can help the primary teachers' subject knowledge'.

I want to finish by reaffirming the fact that while this elephant may be small, it is also very mighty, because it is the foundation on which the education sector is built. In addition to all the aspects that I've mentioned, primary schools hold a special place due to them being the guardians of teaching an invaluable skill: reading. It is the key to every other subject and, in many ways, a key to life. So what better gift can we give a child than the ability to read and a love of reading?

5 A relentless focus on finding and developing talent

People run systems. A school is only as good as its people – the quality of its teachers and support staff. If you cannot recruit and train good people, your organisation is worthless. Having the foresight and confidence to recruit before the need arises is critical; retention is not always the answer. Look for potential. The things that I want in someone are often the things that I can't train someone to have. A person needs to have intellect, be aligned to the mission and be someone who is constantly striving to do things better. This chapter explores how to attract the right people and hire them. We look at the leadership skill of analysis by focusing on staffing structures and managing the subsequent costs. I will also scrutinise individual leadership styles, giving examples along the way. I will introduce you to Simon Cox, a regional education director for a national trust, who has a great perspective on supporting White British boys and developing school culture through sport. My final thoughts are about the advantages of viewing teachers as a commodity and the benefits that this brings to education.

The yarn

Talent can be found in so many places; sadly, we just don't often look for it. You have to make it a deliberate act. Any organisation is only as good as its people. In schools, support staff form a critical role. Like the role of a teacher, without support staff the school falls apart. For me this is crucially important, as they are often the unsung heroes – maybe even more so in secondary than primary. Support staff are not always treated with the respect that they deserve. As someone who comes from a working-class family, I feel that it is extremely important for me to acknowledge this.

My dad worked extremely hard and spent much of his working life cleaning trains. When visiting him as a child during the school holidays, I sometimes went to work with him and loved it. Spending time with him on the night shift, being given the task of looking after the keys and walking on the railway tracks from the station to the parked trains, was heaven for little me. I enjoyed the importance of the role and understood this at an early age. He was a man who understood that hard work gave him a purpose, and he took pride in that. It may seem strange to you – me, here, reminiscing about the awe and wonder that I experienced from the time spent with my dad at work, as people often look down on cleaners. Maybe people out there believe that cleaners have no drive or goals, but they are so key to any business. Let's face it, if you get on a train and it's dirty, you would be somewhat shocked and upset. If you went into a classroom as a teacher, with bins still full, and tables covered in glue and glitter from craft activities that took place the day before, it would be a frustrating start to your day. There are many people who are integral to school life who do important work but whose contributions can often be sadly overlooked. There is sometimes a disregard for the hidden details. A lack of awareness allows individuals to not think about the effort that goes into the unseen. The caretaker who removes obstructions from the environment when they walk into the school every morning. The admin teams who process admissions information consistently and efficiently. The family liaison officer who is supporting a parent on the Phoenix Programme, quietly, in safe spaces. We rely on so many people in schools. The great people who fulfil these roles are not limited to teaching assistants. But teaching assistants are, of course, important too. Those who assist a pupil with SEND (special educational needs and disabilities) to access the learning in the lesson to a high standard, in harmony with the class teacher, are invaluable.

It's important to recognise the value of recruitment because each person in your school plays a role in the development of the culture that you want. I have administrators, financial assistants, IT technicians and the like who have chosen to work in my schools. They could get a job in another school and, on the surface, it would quite easily appear to be no different. A school is a school, right? But they stay for the children and because they buy into the values-based culture. It's important to keep your eyes open, talk to people and remain curious. Sitting behind a desk, attached to a laptop or computer, can prevent you from seeing the people or solutions around you to the issue on which you may be working.

Taking the time to find talent is a good use of this limited resource (time), as talent can be found in a range of places if you are deliberate enough in your actions to discover it. The task of finding talent is one hard task, but developing it is another. As leaders, we also need to be deliberate in this act. Freeing people's time up for development, self-reflection and professional discourse is an element of school life not often mentioned in detail; however, it should be.

Time is a resource that costs money, which is a huge factor to consider in staff development but, organised properly, it is one of the best investments that you will make as a leader. I once watched a teacher deliver a terrible lesson in an interview. The structure was there, he had the knowledge and intellect and he also clearly had the motivation, but he struggled with behaviour management and the session was a car crash. I decided, however, to take a chance on this newly qualified teacher, because I could see that the foundations were there. It was very apparent that he would need to work on his presence and interactions within the classroom, but he had some of the ingredients that all good teachers (or prospective ones) need. He had strong subject knowledge, dedication (he was hard-working) and self-reflection but, most of all, he had the propensity to engage with and learn from feedback. The idea of the little-and-often approach to teacher development was formulating in my head at this time. It was an idea that would turn into the creation of the ProgressTeaching platform, a company of which I am CEO today, which focuses on improving the quality of teaching and learning by looking at teachers' individual needs. I recruited him and it turned out that I made the right choice. Through the support provided over time, he became a teacher who was secure in his practice and continued to grow.

I have always liked to think outside the box, and it was no different when I was looking at how to solve the problem of having the time to offer and deliver high-quality CPD to staff. So I decided to change the school day and the school year. Five inset days became eight. This meant that we were able to have bi-weekly inset sessions after school, focusing on pedagogy and the little-and-often approach. This adaptation to the structure of the school day still included weekly CPD sessions with a subject focus. The arrangement meant that CPD met the individual needs of the teachers. Morning briefings on Mondays (teaching and learning), Wednesdays (pastoral) and Fridays (tutors and curriculum teams) also came into play and gave spaces for the ongoing mini-insets around teaching practices. What these changes offered us was an opportunity. I changed the school year to start at the end of August and finish at the beginning of July, giving more time before external exams and less time after them. I was also able to give teachers non-contact time during marking week, in order for them to work together, moderate and enter into professional discourse for the benefit of the team and the pupils. We were also able to offer increased non-contact time between lessons during the teacher's week, to use at their discretion – they are professionals, after all.

This model isn't cheap – as I said, time is money – but the benefits are evident for the pupils and the staff. Find talent, nurture it and treat people well.

The next conundrums for me to solve were interesting ones: firstly, how to mirror the above example in a primary school? And secondly, how I can make teaching more sustainable? Well, let me ask you this: what would you think about changing to a four-day school week?

'The most valuable resource that teachers have are each other.'

(Robert John Meehan, n.d.)

Leadership skills

Analysis: Detailed examination of anything in order to understand it

I've worked in a variety of London schools. This has given me a powerful perspective. When I first walked into Mossbourne, it became quickly apparent that it was different. Mossbourne was no bog-standard comprehensive. It was a high-performing school and this difference was displayed in a multitude of ways. One of these that stayed with me was the principal's foresight to recruit before the need arose. The first time that I recruited beyond the means of the budget, I was nervous. I'd seen the previous principal use this strategy, year after year, but to do it yourself is a different matter. Using this recruiting strategy for the first time was daunting, as I was looking at the budget wondering whether it would balance in the forthcoming year. The idea of walking into the school year with a deficit budget is not what anyone wants. It never gets easier, but you just need to believe that it will pan out.

Recruitment is a neverending cycle. The normal process of recruitment in a school consists of a person resigning, which triggers an advertisement of the post, and applications. This triggers the shortlisting and results, eventually, in an interview and hopefully the recruitment of someone to replace the person – if all goes to plan, of course. This is the simplified version of the process; quite often, situations don't present themself nicely packaged like this. What if the resignation is handed in at the last minute, leaving no time to find a replacement? Schools can often be left in a panicked, reactive state, trying to find a practitioner when they have missed the peak of the recruitment season.

I don't have to state the obvious, but I will. Leading a MAT as a CEO is very different from leading a school as a principal. Those who know me well also know that I love a whiteboard and drawing out my thinking, as the true mathematician and teacher that I am. As a principal, I held an annual get-together for the extended leadership team to map out the upcoming year, look at the school development plan and review the school budget. In this meeting, I asked my senior and middle leaders what their plan was regarding improving teaching, learning and outcomes, a standing agenda item (which I will revisit in Chapter 6). My dedicated team of leaders all presented as part of their plan the same solution: to retain staff. My response after hearing this for several years was as follows: 'Let's assume that you get your wish and no one leaves. Let's explore that reality.'

The following piece of art is called *The Incremental Drift: The 101 of staffing budgets explained*. For the detail-orientated among you, I have used 2020/21 – 2021/22 Inner London pay scales. The staffing numbers are real (with some slight rounding to make the numbers easier) and from one of my schools.

Everyone on the main scale, M1–M5, moves up one point, approx £2,500.

50 teachers × £2,500 = £125,000

M6 teachers move to UPS 1, approx £4,000.

15 teachers × £4,000 = £60,000

Half the UPS 1 teachers move to UPS 2, approx £1,500.

10 teachers (half the 20 on U1) × £1,500 = £15,000

That's a total of £200,000 (£125,000 + £60,000 + £15,000).
Now let's not forget oncosts (pension and National Insurance) @ approx. 30%

Cost so far: £200,000 + 30% = £260,000

What about senior leaders? We have 27 teachers on the leadership pay scale (all our faculty leads are on leadership pay scale and don't receive TLRs).

Assume half the leaders receive an increment (we have a young staff) 13 × £1,000 = £13,000

Don't forget their pension and NI

£13,000 × 1.3 = £16,900

For a grand total of £276,900

Now you might be lucky and save some money if not all your teachers are in the pension scheme. This will save a few dollars (sorry, pounds – the Australian in me keeps bubbling to the surface). Oh, and don't forget support staff. We have 60 support staff that are critical to the running of the school. Let's assume incremental drift of £23,100 to make the numbers easy. It is much bigger than this in reality. The grand total is £300,000. This assumes no new TLRs (teaching and learning responsibilities). Oh, and don't forget that 2020/21 –21/22 was a zero-percentage pay award year. What if it had been a two per cent pay rise? Much lower than the 2022/23 average of around six per cent when all staff are included. We can add two per cent to our £7,000,000 wage bill and that's another £140,000. Obviously, this doesn't apply to mature schools, where the majority of staff are at the top of the scale, but in that scenario the school has already made all the cuts to the curriculum, staffing and every other budget that they can find. They still need to find the money for any increment drift and cost of living increase, unless their funding increase covers it.

After explaining my masterpiece to the silent group, I continued: 'Therefore, ignoring inflation increases, if there is zero turnover of staff, we need to find approximately £300,000 in year 1, and by year 3 that would be closer to £1 million. (I acknowledge that staff would start to top out of the pay scales, which would reduce the overall cost, but it doesn't change the message.) So where do we get this £1 million from?' You could have heard a pin drop. Does retention drive outcomes? I'll let you ponder that for a bit. My team, on the other hand, quickly realised that their solution of retaining all staff wouldn't work, unless accompanied by a fundamental reorganisation of the curriculum structure to save costs. The state sector is non-profit; therefore, it is an inherent fact that we always need to make savings. Retaining staff can ironically raise more problems to resolve. What are the solutions?

1. **Restructuring and redundancies when staff costs become too high:** This is a cost and still results in people leaving.

2. **Pay people less:** To retain good people you often have to pay them more, and those in education deserve decent salaries.

3. **Larger class sizes, less contact time with a teacher, fewer trips and reduced resources:** This all goes against the many battles that teachers and unions have had to fight in order to improve the education environment for our children.

The solution for me is to have a good teacher turnover of more than 15 per cent, recruit trainee teachers and work hard to retain the best staff. I'm acutely aware of the London-centric nature of this model and the need for it to be adapted to a specific set of circumstances – see points 1, 2 and 3 above for where the compromises might come from.

Scrutiny: Critical observation or examination

The characteristics of leadership are best illustrated in the application of leadership ideas, beliefs and methods. Mintzberg (1998) promoted the idea of the modern leader as 'covert'; he proposes that knowledgeable staff 'respond to inspiration, not supervision' (p. 140). Therefore, a modern leader should not seek to control but to inspire staff unobtrusively and covertly. Mintzberg states that 'many... university professors describe their structures as upside down, with them at the top and with managers on the bottom to serve them'. If one were to apply Mintzberg's beliefs regarding successful leadership to leadership in a successful modern school, one would find a senior team of covert leaders.

There are many frameworks with which to help individuals to become self-aware of their own style of leadership and blind spots. I recommend that they are used, not only for leaders' personal development, but also in order for leaders to understand those around them. However, one should not fall into the trap of thinking that any framework can fully describe a person or their leadership style. They are but a useful guide with which to arrange our thinking.

Oliver Mythodrama (cited by Stebbings and Dopson, 2018) used the four archetypal leaders that can be found in any organisation – the Good King/ Queen, the Warrior/Amazon, the Great Mother/Father and the Medicine Woman/Shaman – to develop Archetypes at Work™ (www.oliviermythodrama. com/archetypes-at-work). Mythodrama argues that leaders have a preferred leadership style, and thus the practice of any given leader will tangibly demonstrate the character qualities associated with their preferred style. The four archetypes are arguably inspired by the work of Swiss psychiatrist Carl Gustav Jung. In their extreme forms, the characters can become the Control Freak, the Bully, the Smotherer or the Change Addict, respectively. At the other end of the characters' spectrum, they become the Abdicator, the Weakling, the Automaton or the Change Resister.

Character	Qualities
Good King/Queen	Rational, strategic, authoritative, attentive to detail, analytic, objective, sets direction
Warrior/Amazon	Competitive, goal-driven, motivating, champion, challenging, risk-taking, determined to win, builds team spirit

Character	Qualities
Great Mother/ Father	Compassionate, emotionally intelligent, reassuring, good listener, builds trust, supportive, open and encouraging, sustains relationships
Medicine Woman/ Shaman	Creative, imagineer, optimistic, visionary, provocateur, experiments, sows seeds

I have selected four characters who are an amalgamation of many leaders from my time in schools to demonstrate the different archetypal leadership characteristics and to show how leadership characteristics can impact personal success or failure. I've also included in the examples any additional impact that covert or overt leadership styles might have on their success. As you read through the four examples, think about yourself, the leaders around you and your team. Which archetypes fit best?

Anna: The Good Queen

Anna has responsibility for curriculum and assessment. Part of her role is ensuring that the academic attainment for all students is accurately assessed and that these assessments are used to improve student outcomes within the school. As well as this, her role includes making sure that there is a well-sequenced and fit-for-purpose curriculum in place. Arguably, the character qualities of the Good Queen are in-built into the job description: Anna is 'analytical, objective and clear' and demonstrates attention to detail. Furthermore, as a trained mathematician, the aforementioned qualities were crucial to Anna's success in her chosen academic pathway.

How do the qualities of the Good Queen manifest themselves in Anna's daily leadership practices?

The good: During the most recent curriculum reforms in the UK, Anna planned and enacted the changes in a strategic way. Anna met with subject leaders to ensure that she understood the implications for each subject and to ensure that she could efficiently implement the curriculum and assessment changes into the whole-school curriculum map, knowledge organisers and assessment calendar. Consequently, Anna implemented the necessary adjustments in an effective and timely fashion.

The bad: However, when presented with an unforeseen change (a change that would support teacher data entry by using a new data-entry system), she adopted the characteristics of the Control Freak (the negative version of the Good Queen). Anna was overcautious and hypercritical of the new system. This caused significant and unnecessary delay to the implementation of the improved data-entry platform.

The ugly: When the Annas of this world convert into the extreme version of the Good Queen, they become the Control Freak and, at the extreme, can suffer from analysis paralysis.

I find the following methods useful when working with a Good Queen or King:

- Use written communication.
- Schedule meetings and one-to-ones to have regular dialogue in a private setting.
- Give clear deadlines.
- Give ample opportunities for them to check expectations of tasks in order to avoid misunderstanding.
- Keep them informed and ensure that they have a voice at wider meetings, where others are often more vocal and confident.
- Use regular, quiet praise.

Remember that Anna is trying to be perfect and do a great job, so approach with compassion and clarity. When Anna operates as an overt leader, she is often ineffective. Essentially, Anna is at her best when perfectly playing the role of the Good Queen and operating as a covert leader. We all know and love an Anna – someone who is exceptionally well planned and diligent but who struggles to adapt to the unplanned.

Dallas: The Great Father

Dallas is responsible for Early Years and safeguarding. In many ways, he is the archetypal Great Father. As with Anna, Dallas's role requires the qualities of his preferred leadership style; Dallas is compassionate, supportive, open and encouraging.

How do the qualities of the Great Father manifest themselves in Dallas's daily leadership practices?

The good: As the lead designated safeguarding leader (DSL) and Early Years leader, Dallas is often required to be open and encouraging when working with children from challenging backgrounds. He works closely with children's social services and other outside agencies to ensure that they understand how best to support children and their families. He constantly holds the senior team, teaching colleagues and the local authority to account, with regard to how to further improve provision for children and safeguarding. The role of lead DSL demands compassion and trust. He must encourage staff and students alike to come forward and speak out. Dallas sets clear direction and expectations for safeguarding practices across the school. Furthermore, his attention to detail is exceptional, especially when ensuring that recordkeeping is accurate, systematic and robust. Within his remit as the safeguarding lead, he must deliver training and disseminate school safeguarding information frequently in a way that is meaningful and accessible. His delivery is both authoritative and clear.

The bad: Due to the emotive nature of the subject of child protection, particularly in Early Years, parents and carers can often feel attacked due to involvement of outside agencies. When this happens, Dallas has the propensity to turn into the Smotherer and adopt the role of the people-pleaser. He holds multiple meetings with parents to try to explain systems and processes in detail, rather than referring things back to the social worker. Historically, in a bid to reach a solution, Dallas has done this at the expense of his own personal time.

The ugly: The Dallases of this world, when leading as the Smotherer, can become too emotionally involved, to the detriment of their own mental health and wellbeing. You will find them regularly working 16-hour days to make up for the time lost to people-pleasing.

I find the following methods useful when working with a Great Father or Mother:

- Give your time.
- Be patient.
- Give them processing time.
- Demonstrate that you trust them by giving them autonomy.
- Encourage them to delegate.

It is Dallas's ability to switch between a covert and overt leadership style that makes him a successful leader. This is exemplified when Dallas undertakes his leadership role for child protection; he explicitly tells people what to do and when to do it, and explicitly reminds them of expectations when they fail to follow protocol. This is in contrast to Dallas at his best as the leader for EYFS, where he operates as a covert leader, and thus questions and probes in a subtle way to get the best outcomes for children. We all know a Dallas, who is compassionate and dependable and puts people at the heart of everything that they do.

Tracy: The Medicine Woman

The religious studies, philosophy and ethics teacher must be a provocateur when debating philosophical discourse and be optimistic when teaching the sometimes divergent ethical constructs applied by different religions. It could be argued that all teachers must embody these qualities; given that Tracy is a practising teacher, it may be assumed that she does. Leaders of teaching and learning, which Tracy is, are assumed to be experimental, imaginative, creative and even provocative – all the features of a Medicine Woman.

How do the qualities of the Medicine Woman manifest themselves in Tracy's daily leadership practices?

The good: As the head of religious studies, one of the first tasks that Tracy undertook was to rewrite all the schemes of learning (the documents outlining what teachers teach). This desire to change things was put to excellent effect when Tracy was required to alter the entire schemes of learning for religious studies in order to meet the expectations of the new curriculum reforms. Tracy demonstrated a creative and visionary approach linked to clear strategic objectives. The end outcome was that the religious studies department grasped the new specifications perfectly. Students' outcomes in religious studies reached an all-time high. Tracy's desire for change as a Medicine Woman had a positive effect.

The bad: Tracy's hunger for change leads her to embrace new technologies, which she often imposes the use of onto the religious studies department, without due consideration. This can often happen on a whim, due to her own excitement about the next new thing. This overt excitement can transform Tracy from the Medicine Woman into the Change Addict.

The ugly: At worst, Tracy can become over-excited; she learns of a new initiative at the weekend and implements it on Monday morning. This leaves staff feeling frustrated, confused and ultimately demotivated, as they perceive the notions as fickle. Tracy's lack of consideration of the impact and unrealistic expectations is at the heart of the Change Addict – the over-played Medicine Woman.

I find the following methods useful when working with a Medicine Woman or Shaman:

- Point them in the right direction.
- Use regular praise.
- Give clear boundaries.
- Give them structure.
- Ensure that a risk–benefit analysis has been undertaken before any change is rolled out.

Tracy can be clear, give directions and set expectations in an overt manner. But when Tracy rushes to implement the latest idea, she is also overt but highly ineffective. It is not Tracy's tendency to be overt that limits her leadership, but the over-playing of the Medicine Woman. She is an overt leader who wears her heart on her sleeve, when she is at both her best and her worst. We all know and love a Tracy, who wants to be involved and solve the problems in a whirlwind, with a lot of creativity, flair and attention.

Leza: The Amazon

Leza's role is to ensure that all operations within the school run effectively. She is responsible for all areas of operations, including compliance, building, premises, etc., and is often given responsibility for new initiatives. Responsibility for systems implies a person with the ability to be analytical with an eye for detail, the character qualities of the Good Queen. The responsibility for new systems implies the ability to think strategically and be clear – further qualities of the Good Queen. Therefore, we might expect Leza to be the Good Queen – but Leza is an athlete and has played sport at a semi-professional level, which would suggest that she is an Amazon. It was her underlying traits of competitiveness, team-building and needing to win at all costs that led to her success as an athlete. On closer inspection, it is these character qualities that push through and drive her and her work.

How do the qualities of the Amazon manifest themselves in Leza's daily leadership practices?

> **The good:** Leza's leadership of sports teams captures the Amazonian instinct. She wants her teams to win at all costs and never neglects to let the staff body know when one of her teams has scored a 'victory'. Furthermore, there have been times when her sportsmanship – especially

when competing (not that anyone else was) – has been questionable. When Leza is presented with a new initiative, the Amazon emerges. Leza is aware of her strengths and weaknesses. She is the master at building a balanced team around a new initiative. For example, she was recently tasked with reviewing and updating the trust's websites. Leza quickly pulled together and coordinated a task force with the right people to look at everything from the trust logo and colours to compliance, a schedule for policy updates, etc. Leza even enrolled someone in her task force to create mission objectives and a Gant chart.

The bad: Leza is very aware that one of her personal weaknesses is attention to detail, and therefore one of the first 'team members' recruited to support the website redesign project was Mary – a member of staff known for having attention to detail. Leza builds her team using staff with essential skills and who are complementary team members. Leza also creates a palpable team spirit. She is never considered the slave driver; staff always want to go above and beyond to help her achieve the task. However, Leza is not always willing to acknowledge others' contributions. This is the Amazon claiming glory for herself.

The ugly: Although Leza can be strategic, this is always in response to a specific goal. Leza leads best when given total autonomy and authority over the task and a clear objective. The Amazon in her will make it happen, no matter what the cost. Leza is not a team player unless she is the captain. She will take risks and has been known to cut corners to achieve the goal, rather than allowing it to reflect negatively on her when the desired outcome is not achieved on time. Without a goal she will always play it safe, preferring not to enter the game and risk failure, or to allow her name to be associated with a failed task. When an initiative is not going smoothly, Leza will do all within her power to ensure that everyone knows she is not responsible for the failure. We see the worst element of the Change Resister's narrow-mindedness, rigidity and blinkered behaviour when Leza is not in control and the task is not her responsibility.

I find the following methods useful when working with an Amazon or Warrior:

- Set clear objectives.
- Assign non-routine tasks.
- Give praise.
- Provide autonomy, with clear check-ins to ensure that corners are not being cut.
- Know the other members of the team and praise them.

We all know and love a Leza, the master covert leader, inspiring staff to give their time voluntarily to her latest cause. However, when Leza is required to be an overt leader – when the task is not her own – she shies away and resists it. This can be to the detriment of the school.

Overt or convert leadership?

The covert leader, as described by Mintzberg (1998), is the most successful of leaders, but the quality of being covert is not in itself a definer of success. Mintzberg (1998) suggests that there is a need for one to adopt the traits of an overt leader when appropriate and necessary. There exist leaders like Dallas, who effortlessly employs the attributes of both covert and overt leadership in order to ensure success. Other leaders, like Tracy, maintain an overt style of leadership and attain varying degrees of success. It is Leza's unwillingness to be overt that ultimately limits her success. Anna's leadership suffers from her absolute intractability to shift from the leadership style in which she is most comfortable. Therefore, a leader's success is not dependent on being consistently covert, but is dependent on the leader's ability to adapt and adopt the style to suit the relevant situation, climate and environment.

The four archetypal leaders that Mythodrama describes are not different from Mintzberg's overt and covert styles of leadership; it is a leader's ability to transcend and switch between the 'types' that ensures success. Ultimately, it is a leader's ability to adopt their preferred style flawlessly, combined with an ability to effortlessly adopt one of the other styles (as and when necessary) that makes an exceptional leader.

Case study: Simon Cox, MAT Regional Education Director (Secondary and Primary), England

Introduction

Simon, for me, is someone who represents what it means to have a child-centred approach. His determination on ensuring that children feel that they belong is unshakeable. He introduced me to the concept of advocates for children in receipt of the pupil premium grant (PPG). This means not just having a PPG lead but also having an individual who looks at all aspects of school life through the lens of equity for PPG pupils.

Case study

This case study looks at Simon Cox's journey and offers advice from him for leaders who want to make sustainable and future-proof improvements to their schools. Simon has a long track record of success, which started in 2014 at Woodlands School in Basildon, Essex. In his first month, 58 staff left. The school had 45 per cent of its students categorised as PPG and 89 per cent as White British, and its outcomes were in the lowest ten per cent of schools in the country. It also had a privately funded initiative (PFI) building, which brought with it its own cost implications.

Within four years of Simon being in post, the school had a monitoring visit from Ofsted and a full Section 5 inspection. The outcome of the full inspection was extremely positive. Simon had moved Woodlands from 'requires improvement' to 'good' with 'outstanding' features in behaviour and leadership. Given the context of the school, its size and its location, Simon chose to embark on an elite sports programme and managed to rank number four in the country against the likes of Eton and Harrow. By the time he left in 2019, the school was 65 per cent oversubscribed. It received 496 first-choice applications for the 300 available places.

After the success at Woodland's, Simon went on to continue his journey by becoming a headteacher in a school that was a part of a national MAT. His school in Daventry had always been 'requires improvement' or 'special measures' and it had accumulated 286 days of exclusion in just one term before he joined. But Simon came with a fresh approach. Within two years, the school had a full Section 5 inspection, where it was awarded 'outstanding' for leadership and behaviour, with a grading of 'good' overall. Cox was able to achieve this during the COVID pandemic, which is no easy feat. It's no wonder that Simon was appointed the MAT Regional Director for the South in 2021.

In 2021, he was asked to be the executive head of Danetre Southbrook Learning Village (DSLV), an all-through school in Daventry. You guessed it – it was in a bit of a pickle as well. Within 18 months, in March 2022, DSLV had a Section 5 inspection and it was rated a solid 'good', from

A relentless focus on finding and developing talent

reception through to sixth form. It's clear that Simon is a highly skilled leader, who has a tested and proven framework for rapidly turning schools around. Every time I speak to Simon, his mission radiates from him; he truly believes that children deserve the best from their school and their teachers. He believes that the work that he's done at the schools is what the children deserve; it is one of the ingredients of his success. Turning a school around is a significant achievement; turning multiple schools around is astonishing.

Simon demonstrates his aptitude for constantly learning and improving himself while drawing on his experiences, because every school is different. His framework for success is his ABCDE model. It helps him to identify what needs to be done:

- **Assess:** One size doesn't fit all. What worked at a previous school won't necessarily work at the current school. You need to understand the unique challenges that your particular school is facing and what needs to change.
- **Behaviour:** At every school Simon's been to, behaviour has been an issue at the start. This has been for different reasons. At one school, the children misbehaved because there weren't systems in place to help them to move forwards. In another school, it was down to the fact that the teaching wasn't up to scratch, so the children messed about.
- **CPD:** CPD is crucial for staff buy-in. Teachers need to be appreciated and have their career goals supported. Give them the opportunity to develop, visit other schools, get on an NPQ (national professional qualification) programme and get that promotion that they deserve when they're being the teacher that their pupils need them to be.
- **Direction:** This is about the culture. At one school, for example, the culture was quite oppressive. This needed to change so that staff knew that it was important to be kind and supportive to each other, as well as to their pupils. Having taken other schools on this journey, Simon can recognise where a school is and set landmarks to track how they are improving. It's important that you involve families in this too. One of the first things that Simon does is have a parent forum, so that he can listen to their frustrations and work with them moving forwards.

- **Energy:** Bring positive energy and your team will feed off it. As leaders, we're also trying to create the next generation of leaders. We need to share our insights with the teaching community so that our work can be continued after we've left, and our schools can constantly improve.

Simon also has tips (3 Rs) that are clear for prospective or current headteachers with whom he works:

Recruitment: That's staff and students. The recruitment of staff is key, not only to have bodies in the classroom but also to have the right people that buy into your vision. The more students you get, the more opportunities you get. This then leads to an increase in the budget. It's like a restaurant being full – word of mouth spreads, and everyone wants to go there once they see that it's always full.

Results: You need to deliver those outcomes at GCSE, Year 6 and A levels. Results are a key indicator of how well you're doing as a school.

Relationships: All this links back to relationships with staff, pupils and your local community. Good relationships are so important if you want people to support you and be with you on your journey of improvement.

The solution

Teacher recruitment is like the football transfer window. The teacher has already decided to move, so you have a limited window of opportunity. On numerous occasions I've seen leaders go out, recruit before a position is available and hedge their bets. As an example of this, imagine that you have a science department of 20 people. In London, it wouldn't be a bad assumption to make that one of those 20 people might resign to move abroad, because of lifestyle changes, because they want a promotion that you can't offer or because they've realised that the school culture just isn't for them. You know this because you have years of information and knowledge, so why not recruit before the need arises when the market is at its best? I advertise in January for jobs in September that don't exist yet. Bold move? No. Great leaders are not risk-averse. There is a big difference between calculated risk and being reckless. There needs to be an ongoing analysis of risk across many areas of the school; however, leaders often forget that this includes staffing.

'What if no one resigns?' I hear you ask. Well, using the example of the science teacher, you could be looking at a £60k deficit or the staff members in the department might wobble upon seeing the advertisement and think that someone is being managed out. I'm sure that you are beginning to see, as you read through the chapters, the role that culture plays in underpinning everything. Let me explain *how* in more detail before we leave this chapter.

- **The worry that no one resigns, you are overstaffed and in a deficit budget:** Look at the risk: bigger departments hold less risk than a smaller department in a secondary school and, therefore, it is a rational recruitment strategy. £60,000 is a reasonable risk in a £10 million-plus budget.

- **The worry that someone is being managed out:** You develop an open culture regarding teacher development: leaders ask annually at key points of the academic year whether staff are considering leaving. They can then have an open discussion with the leaders, who offer support in helping them to move into their next role, be that at the school or elsewhere. A culture of openness and honesty about the quality of every single teacher's practice ensures that there are no surprises.

The final words

There is an assumption that staff retention is the ultimate goal. As a CEO not only of a MAT but also of a start-up company, I believe that retention is vitally important, but not at all costs. For example, if a client support person wants to leave my software company, I really do want and need them to stay, because they often have years of information in their head and only a few people understand the technical elements of the product. They are completely in tune with the company culture and the software. However, even in this example, the knowledge that they hold needs to be balanced against the cost.

It's important to understand that all jobs have been commoditised, to varying degrees. I have a sweet tooth – many of us do, and as a result, many companies harvest and refine sugar, such as Südzucker AG, Tate and Lyle, and Sunshine Sugar to name a few. For all intents and purposes, the product that they produce is the same. Ultimately, it's all still sugar. The only differentiator is the type of sugar: brown, castor, white, raw… do you see where I'm going? We need to look at the elements of teaching (the teacher) that have been commoditised.

Teachers in the UK, as in many countries, have been commoditised like sugar. There is a minimum level of criteria necessary to be called a teacher and there are different types of teachers: maths, English, primary, Early Years… the list goes on. It is this commoditisation of teaching that separates it from many professions and ultimately lowers the cost of training a new hire. Think about it this way: it would take me weeks to train a new customer services person in my software company before I could let them loose on a customer – even if they've worked at customer services before at another company. They would need to learn a minimum amount of technical knowledge about the product and understand the company culture before they can answer a single client question. Yet we let a teacher loose on a class with often little more than a day of training from your organisation. This is only achievable because teaching has a high degree of commoditisation. It is due to this fact that we as an industry need to stop comparing ourselves to and looking at research from other fields when it comes to retention. In the long run, the cost of losing a person and training a new hire is significantly lower in education than in a lot of other industries.

When a teacher has decided to leave and you are recruiting a replacement to come into your school, you are asking yourself how much training is needed, within a fixed period of days, to get them up to speed. This is the risk–benefit analysis. Therefore, when recruiting a replacement teacher, I look for things that can't be commoditised, like intellect, alignment to the mission and constantly striving to do things better. Intellect is not about being an intellectual; it's about capacity to learn, subject knowledge and wherewithal. We design our interview process to capture these elements because it is these things that separate the great teachers from the average ones.

Top tips

- Recruit before the need arises.
- Design your recruitment processes to capture the elements of teaching that haven't been commoditised.
- Use archetypes to support you in understanding yourself and your team.

A well looked-after elephant

Aha. You've found another one! You are good at this.

At this point, I think that it is important to make a comment about the value and the role of the pastoral system in a school. Education is a relationship-based profession after all. I also need to let you know that this important elephant comes with a trigger warning.

There was a period of time when my schools were considered the strictest in England. The title is currently bestowed upon another great principal, doing some great work with and for children. Mossbourne was set up at a time when the state of education in Hackney was dire. It was a dreadful period in history, when the local authority had been stripped of its power to run education for the borough due to monumental failings that would have repercussions for years to follow. Hackney Downs School, the school named in the Houses of Parliament as the 'worst school in the country', was closed during this period. Mossbourne was built on the ashes of Hackney Downs. How would you feel as a child, carer, parent, teacher or community member if this was being said about your school and your local authority? And what impact do you think going to the worst school in the country would have on your education as a child, let alone your self-esteem and sense of worth?

Hackney's education offer was so dire after the school closure that children who had attended Hackney Downs were sent to schools in the borough with worse GCSE outcomes. (Please read this again for me before you continue.) I tell you this because if there is anyone who truly believes that the success we have achieved as a federation did not include and sit firmly on the foundations of the utmost care and love for every single one of our pupils – past, present and future – then they really don't understand what it takes to work with young people and help them to excel in mind, body and spirit. They therefore, in my opinion, have no validity to their argument or self-assumed conclusions. Children don't try for or learn from people with whom they don't have a rapport. Period.

Yes, I truly believe that the work is in finding balance, and yes, sometimes there are slight exceptions to the rule, on which I will elaborate shortly. I feel that when the pastoral element controls the school, the outcomes of children go backwards and the schools don't quite feel right. When the instruction, teaching and learning take over, it doesn't feel right either. The perfect storm lies in the tension where the pastoral team and the academic team champion their areas, like gladiators (who make up over coffee in the staffroom afterwards), fighting for the acknowledgement that their area of expertise is the most important for our children. The principal is the one who decides on the victor of each battle of wills. This should be a constant battle (aka healthy and professional debate) in any great leadership team.

Children in our Hackney community die. Children in our Hackney community are often routinely stopped under Operation Trident. Children in our Hackney community are strip-searched and subjected to adultification in presumed places of safety. I am very aware that these are three very powerful statements, but they are true and they are every carer's, parent's, teacher's, principal's, CEO's and community's worst nightmare. It is something that we cannot and will not ignore.

The children in our primary and secondary schools play. This sounds like a given but it's not, when going to a park or crossing postcodes can put you at risk. Our rules, systems and expectations mean that children can be children the moment in which they step over the line and into our areas of safety. I can categorically state that children can be themselves within our walls and we will protect that right for them. There is an expectation that any bravado is left on the pavements outside. We see them and understand our context, and as a result, our children excel in many, many ways.

As of 2023, Local Crime in Context states that the crime rate in Hackney is 14 per cent higher than the average in London and 30 per cent higher than the average in England, Wales and Northern Ireland's overall figure. Hackney is in the top five most dangerous boroughs in London (Crime Rate UK, 2023). I return to the earlier comment, regarding there being some exceptions to the rules. There are exceptions – the ones when you sink deeply into the true nature of pastoral care. They are the situations about which I will never talk in detail outside of our community, due to the respect and care that I have for individuals, but as a leader I say this for your benefit. My wish for you is that nothing terrible happens to a child in your school or a young person who once attended. I have grieved with families in our communities. I have felt the losses and held the hands of individuals for whom I would have done anything to take away the pain that will sit within them forever. We are unapologetic in our ambitions for our children. Our mission, to create environments where learning is the norm, is what it is for a very good reason.

I end this elephant ride by talking about my big brother, Andrew. My sister called him Roo when she was little, because she couldn't say his full name, and it stuck. Roo was a slightly more golden, chiselled version of me and grew to the amazing height of 6'5". He was a beautiful young man. He had settled in Sydney for some years by the time I finished university, but he was still tormented by our past. The pastoral support that he needed throughout his childhood was never afforded to him, and he was never really able to get out from under the clouds of his experiences as a consequence. When I think of him, my mind sees us riding bikes as young boys and the impressive stunts that he would pull off, him cooking me toast, and us swimming in the local watering hole. I know that I do this because that's how I want to remember him. My big brother Andrew died in police custody at the age of 25, in a Sydney police station. There was the usual inquiry that happens when there is a death in custody. It provided no real answers and to this day, my family and I still don't know the full details of what happened that night. What I do know is that my brother was picked up for petty theft, refused bail (having previously missed several court appearances) and detained. Roo didn't leave the police station alive. No parent should have to bury their child, but my mum did. He was taken from us too soon.

At its simplest, the pastoral provision in a school is the essential foundation for learning. It removes barriers for the most vulnerable and is crucial for children's physical and emotional welfare, especially for those who could easily find themselves lost. Never underestimate its importance. I certainly don't.

6 Teaching and learning above all

It speaks for itself: the quality of the teaching is the foundation and strength of a school. Great schools have consistently good teaching, day in, day out. For a disadvantaged child, the difference between a good and a bad teacher is monumental. Research shows that the quality of teaching is by far the biggest factor within schools that impacts on the achievement of children, especially those from poorer backgrounds. Within this chapter, I look at teaching and learning as a science, and at the leadership skills of research and background, by looking at the work of leading charities who focus on improving outcomes for children across the United Kingdom. I will introduce you to Mohsen Ojja, CEO of a large MAT with 16 schools across multiple regions in England. Mohsen is passionate about and highly skilled in understanding teaching and learning and knows what it takes to develop it. In my final thoughts, I offer my views on the importance of developmental coaching in schools.

The yarn

60:20:20. This is how a school budget is approximately split. Sixty per cent on teaching staff, 20 per cent on support staff and 20 per cent on everything else.

The core business of education is teaching and learning. High-quality teaching equals outcomes for children (outcomes can be expressed in many different ways, as seen with Mossbourne's many artefacts). As a leader or an aspiring leader, how often are you actually talking about our core business? Honestly, it really isn't a trick question. I'm very aware of the noise (as discussed in Chapter 2) that can distract individuals from the ultimate and most important focus: teaching and learning. Schools are spending 70 per cent of their budget, if not more, directly on classroom practice. If leaders are not talking about teaching and learning on a weekly basis in great detail, they should be.

The academisation programme began under the Labour government in the early 2000s. It was originally used to target struggling schools in more deprived areas. Academisation was used to give schools more control over their finances and their curriculum. It broke the link between schools and local authorities, with academies receiving their funding directly from central government instead of through a local council. At the time of the Conservative and Liberal Democrat coalition government in 2010, the academisation programme went into overdrive. Schools judged 'outstanding' were given the opportunity to sever ties with the local authority and convert to academy status.

At the beginning of the academy movement, as more academies appeared in England, there was an ongoing media frenzy about the changing landscape of educational establishments. Leaders of these new academies were regularly approached by the media. They gave all kinds of statements about how unique and wonderful their academy would be. Academies, at this time, were all about changing the status quo. Some leaders declared that the classroom environment needed to be revolutionised; I went to one school where classrooms only had three walls, with all classes being open to the central atrium. Imagine being a maths teacher, trying to get your class to do some quiet independent work, while the class next door are doing a marketplace activity with students moving from stall to stall to stall – mayhem. Others boasted of a project-based curriculum, drop-down days or a learning-to-learn approach (metacognition).

When my principal was approached at the time of academisation for his comments regarding what he would be doing differently for his academy, he informed them of his strategy, which was simply (but not so simple) '**to teach well**'. A leader's focus on the quality of teaching and learning is paramount.

How does this fit with my view on retention?

I was at a conference a short while ago and a leader said loud and proud that retention is the key. It was presented as the magic wand to all problems. Now they had obviously not seen my diagram from Chapter 5 at this point, but you have, so you are aware of my viewpoint on this. Retention of the right people is key. However, overall, general retention, which creates incremental drift that impacts negatively on organisational growth, is dangerous if other factors are not considered.

I, of course, being me, asked the question: 'How did this leader combat the growth and unsustainable budget increases of retaining staff who cost more and more each year?' The response was: 'We promote them.' I resisted the urge to scream out my follow-up question, which was 'where do all these jobs come from?' If all the great people are getting promotions, somebody must be leaving. The only people that could be leaving in this scenario are the people at the top. Is the principal leaving or is it the CEO? I couldn't help but think of the nursery rhyme 'Ten in the bed' as I kept my thoughts to myself.

There were ten in the bed
And the little one said,
'Roll over! Roll over!'
So, they all rolled over
And one fell out...

Quality-first teaching is the answer to all the questions, and staff movement can strengthen that. We discussed staff movement in the previous chapter, but I say it again: don't be afraid of it. In schools where staff mobility is low, all is not lost; this presents a different challenge, when principals are faced with individuals who won't or don't want to develop and grow. If you are standing still in education, you are actually moving backwards. The tide moves regardless, so you need to keep moving forwards. That requires you to be deliberate in your approach to improving teaching and learning.

ProgressTeaching

I created ProgressTeaching to bring observations, pupil progress information and appraisals together in one place. It was a shock to me that no one else had attempted to do this before. It was a huge task, yes, but not at all impossible, especially when you have a great group of people to work with in developing it. In education, people can often make assumptions regarding who the great teachers are in a school. Sometimes it is based on a one-off amazing observation and sometimes it's based on the practitioner's presence in the classroom and around the school. But we all know that perceptions shouldn't override the facts, which ought to be based on the outcomes of the children whom they teach. Great teaching is evidenced in the progress that children make from their various starting points and the support that they receive for their needs. Schools need to embody a culture of continuous professional development to get the best out of everyone. Great professional development is linked to the needs of the teacher, the children and the school. For example, watching a lesson without having any idea of the curriculum intent is like writing an essay without knowing the question. An essay needs to answer a question in the same way that a teacher needs to know the curriculum and the class context in order to teach well. For clarity, I'm not saying that you can't observe and provide feedback to a teacher if you don't know the curriculum, but we need to understand the limitations. If the intent and the implementation are not linked, what is the point to the lesson?

At Mossbourne, we break down the elements of teaching into habits. In our secondary schools, we adopted the primary school approach to data in Key Stage 3 because it works, and it means that our language around data is accessible. All our teachers understand these grades for children: Developing, Foundation, Secure, Advanced and Excellent. These are understandable by all teachers in a way that GCSE grades 2+, 3+ and so on are not in Key Stage 3. The power in this approach for coaching and mentoring is that it allows teachers to observe a lesson and check children's levels of understanding in that moment, because our assessment system is directly linked to our curriculum statements.

Introducing this structure of support and development allowed us to identify and scrutinise our own practice as leaders. I knew that if we wanted great teaching, we needed to provide high-quality support and CPD, and this idea was further reinforced when we had some bad Year 13 results in a subject one year. When presented with this, the first question that I asked was, 'What did the observations tell us about the practice in those classes?' Guess what? I didn't get a response because we hadn't observed the teachers' Year 13 practice all year. There was no escaping the truth: we had to look at ourselves. This wasn't a teacher issue; it was a leadership issue. As leaders, we needed to maintain an open dialogue with staff that included providing feedback and development opportunities, but we had failed at this task.

You may encounter times when someone wants you, as the principal, to put a teacher on a support plan or when leaders are complaining about a teacher's practice in an SLT meeting. When presented with these situations, the first question that you should ask is: Who has told the teacher and what does the record say? If the record hasn't made it clear to the teacher that there is an issue, then there is a leadership issue, and not a teacher one. There might be a support plan, but it's not the teacher that needs one. We are quick in education to blame the teacher. However, we need to understand what the leaders have done to mentor and coach staff and whether they have done everything possible to develop that individual. If they can't say yes, then it's time to look at how you can upskill your leadership team in order for them to be equipped with the skills to bring out the best in the teachers around them. It shouldn't be a rare act to look at the quality of teaching alongside learning and pupil progress and attainment data. And it shouldn't be a rare act to offer coaching and mentoring to our colleagues on a regular basis for the benefit of both them and their pupils.

Leadership skills

Research: The collecting of information about a particular subject

There is a lot of research in education. I have personally found that the Sutton Trust, a charity that aims to improve social mobility and address educational disadvantage in the UK, and the Education Endowment Foundation (EEF), which aims to reduce the link between family income and education outcomes in England, are excellent sources of information when it comes to teaching and learning. Both charities were set up by educational philanthropist Sir Peter Lampl OBE.

The Sutton Trust reports

The Sutton Trust reports 'Improving the impact of teachers on pupil achievement in the UK – interim findings' (2011a) and 'What makes great teaching?' (Coe et al., 2014) offer some interesting insight into the idea of teaching and learning above all. I do not present these as the only pieces of research, but these were significant reports for me personally, and contained themes that have been revisited numerous times in subsequent research.

Teacher impacts

The two factors from the 2011 Sutton Trust report that still resonate with me today are:

- The difference between a good and bad teacher for a pupil from a disadvantaged background is a year of learning. That is 0.5 years of learning with a bad teacher compared to 1.5 years of learning with a good teacher.
- We need to observe teachers to predict how effective they might be.

Why do these factors resonate with me? As someone who grew up disadvantaged, this piece of research speaks to my lived experience. I am also aware of the confirmation bias within my statement. That said, this is research, and we can never lose sight of the obvious. What feels like a truism is that great teachers are important. They are even more important for pupils from disadvantaged backgrounds.

What does this mean in practice?

In my schools, up to 50 per cent of the children can be from a disadvantaged background; therefore, it is my moral imperative, in a way that wouldn't be true if I were the principal of a private school, to ensure that my students have good teachers in front of them every single day. I recall a talk – forgive me, as I cannot attribute this to its owner as it was so long ago – where a presenter said that 'a bad teacher in a secondary school affects 150 students' learning every day' (assuming 30 students across five classes a day). When we allow a bad teacher to remain in one of our schools, we are failing hundreds of children every day. This was further reinforced by the Education Endowment Foundation in 'The EEF guide to the pupil premium' (EEF, 2022), where the number one approach to improving outcomes for the most disadvantaged was named as high-quality teaching.

The second point that I take from the 2011 Sutton Trust report is that we can only predict whether someone is going to be a good teacher by observing them. This point begs a very simple question: how do we know when we've seen good teaching? What does the research tell us about what improves student outcomes? The 2014 Sutton Trust report states that content knowledge (this is part of what I call intellect in Chapter 5) and quality of instruction are the key factors of great teaching. The report goes on to highlight the elements that underpin the quality of teaching practice as being: effective questioning, use of assessment, reviewing previous learning, giving pupils model responses, time for practice and scaffolding new learning.

The report also highlights seven commonly used teaching strategies that are not supported by evidence, including: use of lavish praise for low-attaining students; discovery learning; ability groups (although I must confess that I am a staunch believer in setting and that setting makes it easier for teachers to be good teachers – I recommend reading *Reassessing 'Ability' Grouping* by Francis et al., 2020); rereading and highlighting as a learning tool; raising confidence in a topic before teaching it; preferred learning styles; and active learning rather than listening passively. For me, it's just as important to have clarity on what is unsupported by research – and therefore unlikely to have an impact – as it is to know what does work and is shown to have an impact. I am always on the lookout for things that we can stop doing. How else do we fit in everything that we 'should be doing'?

At this moment, I feel that it's important to bring forward something that Dylan Wiliam said in a talk at the Inspiring Leaders Leadership Conference in 2022 (https://inspiringleaderstoday.com). Often, educational research has been misconstrued and destroyed by the time that it gets to the classroom. He offered up the well-known example of teachers putting students' names on ice cream sticks and placing them in a pot, ready to select when asking questions during the lesson. The original intent of the practice was based on research that suggested 'High-engagement classroom environments appear to have a significant impact on student achievement' (Wiliam, 2017 p.126). The concept is that every child would need to be listening and thinking about the answer, because their name might be chosen from the pot. There are now several adaptations of this concept, which you may see in classrooms, that miss the intent of the original idea and its link to the research.

One example of this is when the teacher asks the question, selects the stick and the child answers the question. All is as it should be so far; however, at this point, the teacher now places the 'used' stick aside, rather than putting it back into the pot. This allows the child who answered the question to switch off, relax and disengage. They know that they will not be called upon again to answer subsequent questions in that session. Another example is when the teacher selects the stick, reads the child's name aloud and then asks the intended question. Obviously, at this point only one child must pay attention; this is not to say that the other children will disengage or that a second stick may not be chosen from the pot, but again the original intention has been lost.

I use Wiliam's point here not to berate teachers or to point fingers, but to emphasise that the essence of a practice and its link to research can easily be lost. As leaders, we need to make sure when implementing a research-based strategy that the original research, methodology and intended purpose are shared with our teachers and leaders to ensure that they understand the 'why' of the strategy and, ultimately, that they implement strategies that are aligned to the original research. As Wiliam has done with his suggested use for ice cream sticks. All too often in my career I've seen schools and leaders swayed by the latest trend; in the worst cases, these trends have zero basis in research. The most famous of these was visual, auditory and kinaesthetic (VAK) learning styles. They were all the rage when I first came to the UK. I recall my school having a whole day's inset on this approach and me being provided with questionnaires to use in all my classes to assess every child's learning style. VAK was the height of pseudoscience in education and has since been debunked and thrown on the scrap heap, where it belongs.

Preferred teaching styles still exist and are often presented as beneficial, despite having no basis in research to suggest that they improve student outcomes. I rarely find a teaching and learning leader, principal or inspector who doesn't think that children should be active participants in learning.

They believe that the children will learn more and remember more as active learners. This active learning takes many forms: group work, discovery learning, think/pair/share – the list goes on. The Sutton Trust report 'What makes great teaching?' (Coe et al., 2014) clearly identified active learning as having no discernible measurable benefit on student outcomes. Not all things are good or bad, but we can't present neutral things as being beneficial or insist that people do them.

Other trends have a firm basis in fact (ice cream sticks) but have lost the essence of the underlying research as they are passed from person to person to person. Leaders and teachers need to ensure that we understand the original concept, idea and reasoning of research before we implement it into classrooms, or we run the risk of introducing pseudoscience.

The two Sutton Trust reports highlight the importance of the teacher, what makes great teaching and the fact that you can only predict a teacher's effectiveness through observations. In a lot of ways, this is telling us what works and what doesn't, but the question that I'm left asking myself is: How do we turn this into actionable insight? Within Chapter 4, I discussed the implementation of a high-frequency, low-stakes developmental model for improving teaching and learning practices, but as you can see here, we need to be clear on what instructional skills and attributes we are looking to develop in our teachers. The teaching and learning leads in my schools have turned these key components of good instruction from research into a framework of habits of good teaching. This is not a checklist from the good old days, but a tool with which to frame discussions, set next steps and recognise great practice to be shared.

I'm aware that the world is divided on the concept of grading lessons; as previously stated, I don't think that it's valuable to grade a lesson. I think that, at best, grading a lesson is an aggregation of all of the pedagogy seen. As with all aggregation, the important detail can often be hidden or lost. Let's imagine the new teacher who diligently plans their lessons and marks all of their books to inform the next day's practice, but who struggles with behaviour and routines. In this example, we would find that the overall grade of the lesson would be dragged down by the teacher's struggles in this one particular area. The nuances of the teacher's instruction and developmental needs, and possibly those of the department and the school, is lost to the aggregation. However, if we were to evaluate the different elements of the lesson, we would find that our new teacher is effective at feedback and questioning but that their behaviour and routines are still developing, and we would not penalise them for it. Applying this evaluative approach to instruction in this way allows you to quickly identify the areas of need for an individual, department, subject, school or even across multiple schools.

We need to be honest with ourselves. As leaders, when looking at elements of a lesson, we are always asking ourselves: Is this effective practice? Is this a highly effective practice that needs to be shared? Is this an area of development for this teacher? Whether or not we record our evaluation and share it with the teacher is a moot point. Leaders are constantly evaluating what they see. Why not share what we are already thinking with the teacher? These evaluations and their aggregation can then be used to identify good practice and areas for development. As leaders, we can then create strategic plans that will improve the quality of instruction for an individual, a department, a subject, a school or a group of schools. You may think that this is covert grading of lessons, but I disagree. The narrow focus on a particular element and the removal of Ofsted language, replacing it with what is effective in my school or MAT, makes it fundamentally different.

Background: The circumstances or situation prevailing at a particular time or underlying a particular event

Would you like to live in a meritocratic society?

If you really want to understand how important teaching and learning is, look no further than the admission rates to our top universities for state school and disadvantaged children. Only 150 schools/colleges – approximately five per cent – account for over half the entrants to Oxford and Cambridge, according to a House of Commons briefing paper (Bolton, 2021). It's clear that there is a belief that universities charging higher tuition fees have an obligation to support access to university for underrepresented groups (Office for Fair Access, 2018), but what has changed and for whom?

Progress has been made, as the gap between those least likely and those most likely to attend a top university 'is smaller than ever before' (UCAS, 2017). This was backed up by the Sutton Trust report (2021), which stated that 'at the most selective Russell Group universities (Oxbridge, plus LSE and Imperial College) the proportion of FSM-eligible students had risen from 1.7% to 2.2% in 2018–19' (p. 4); acceptance rates are slightly higher at the less selective Russell Group universities.

A Sutton Trust report (2011b) identified that state school students from the best boroughs are ten times more likely to gain access to a top university and

50 times more likely to gain access to Oxbridge than students from Hackney. However, in recent times we've seen a significant increase in the number of children from the London boroughs of Hackney and Newham attending Oxbridge. This increase sat alongside an increase in the academic outcomes for children from these boroughs and across London in general. What is clear is that the rates of admissions for state school pupils to Oxford (67 per cent) and Cambridge (68 per cent) is higher than ever before (Bolton, 2021). In 2019, due to continued pressure to increase diversity within Oxbridge, they announced in a combined effort that they would be offering free foundation year programmes. The programmes were and still are targeted at disadvantaged students who were offered a place but who struggled to meet the entry requirement or needed help with the transition to Oxbridge (Busby, 2019).

What is the message?

In England, independent school pupils are seven times more likely to gain a place at Oxford or Cambridge compared to those in non-selective state schools, and over twice as likely to take a place at Russell Group institutions (Montacute and Cullinane, 2018). I do not believe that wealthy private school students are seven times more 'able' than state school students or 50 times more able than children receiving free school meals. It is time for change.

The interventions and support that The Elephant Group (www.theelepha ntgroup.org) provide are designed to enable students to attain the required standards. Oxford, Cambridge and many other universities have always been clear that students need to obtain the required academic standard in order to be successful and to gain access to their undergraduate courses. The programme, provided by The Elephant Group, is driven in schools by great teachers who understand the significance of focusing on teaching and learning above all and the positive impact that this can have on mobility for their students. The in-school expert is responsible for selecting, with the support of The Elephant Group, the most appropriate intervention and support for each student.

This brings to life the critical importance of good teaching and learning, especially in areas of high deprivation. Without good teaching, we are never going to change the face of our most prestigious universities and, ultimately, society. A great education is a golden key that unlocks a child's future. With '43% of state secondary school teachers say[ing] they would rarely, or never, advise their bright pupils to apply to Oxbridge' (Sutton Trust, 2016) it is clear that organisations like The Elephant Group working with children on accessing the top universities must extend beyond the student – and they have. Matt Jones, who has written the foreword for this book, is the founder of The Elephant Group, a charity dedicated to using its knowledge to support state schools and their students in accessing the top universities. In 2022, 54 per cent of The Elephant Group cohort from across England gained a place at a 'top third' university.

Why is it important?

I don't agree that everyone should go to university. Most of my own family didn't choose to go and have still been highly successful. Some have taken up a trade, while others are stock and station agents or have gone into the care profession. I think that a plumber is just as important in society as a doctor. We call both in an emergency. However, what I do believe and advocate for is to create a path where young people have a choice. A genuine choice, where they can decide whether they want to go to Oxbridge or to become an electrician – or both.

> *'If you come from a disadvantaged background, we all know that you're much less likely to get good GCSEs and A levels than your more advantaged peers. And those who do get into university are more likely to drop out, less likely to get a first or 2:1, and less likely to find professional level employment. At every stage of their education, the window of opportunity closes a little.' (Office for Students, 2023)*

When young people have had a great education, they are more likely to get the top jobs and higher salaries and have social mobility, or all three. Young people from low-income homes are four times more likely to become socially mobile if they go on to higher education (Sutton Trust, 2021).

Who is this question for?

You: the reader.

Case study: Mohsen Ojja, MAT CEO (secondary and primary), England

Introduction

I met Mohsen many years ago through a mutual friend (Glen Denham). We had all been part of the Future Leaders programme and moved into headships. Mohsen spent the majority of his own schooling in France, speaks at least three languages. As someone who moved to the UK and entered into teaching by chance after completing a law degree, he brings a unique perspective on educational leadership to the English system. Mohsen's aptitude for school improvement has been demonstrated multiple times. His impact on education and improving the life chances of children has, as a result, been widespread and hugely positive for the communities that he has served and continues to serve.

Case study

Essentially, no educational organisation can be better than the quality of the instruction that is happening in the classroom – this was the knowledge that I took with me when I was appointed as principal of The Crest Academy (Crest) in North West London. I arrived at the academy and set out to make a change to the existing culture by putting teaching and learning at the heart of its transformation. I started in January 2015, and at the time Crest was two schools, divided by gender. Both the girls' and boys' schools had serious weaknesses, but the boys' school was worse and had received an Ofsted judgement that placed it into special measures. It was very clear that the boys' school was dysfunctional. Fundamentally, the children were not getting the right provision or instruction, so they were not able to make the appropriate progress in their learning.

It is one thing to be able to identify the weaknesses of a provision, but you then have to put in place measures to change it. When it came to Crest, there was a huge amount of variation and discrepancy between classes and, due to the volatile environment within the academy, it needed structure. The first pressing matter was setting a clear vision and providing a clear set of expectations of what I believed needed to happen in every single classroom. To ensure that we were all singing from the same hymn sheet, I formulated a basic set of non-negotiables that I needed to see in every lesson. These non-negotiables were a fairly basic set of expectations: every teacher would meet and greet the students at the beginning of the lesson, would provide students with a thoughtful 'do now' activity to ensure that the class were settled and ready to learn, would plan lessons that included 'two boxes' (one where the activities would be adapted for pupils who needed support and another for those who needed stretch and challenge), would ensure that every lesson had a plenary and, finally, would dismiss classes in a particular way. While this may seem like common practice for many teachers, this was not the case when I first arrived at Crest.

It was then time to ensure that staff were aligned with the new vision. Now when taking on a new school, setting the vision and the expectation is the easy part. You arrive at the school with a set of fundamental principles and you can talk about them until the cows come home. The real hard part is ensuring that every leader – and I mean every leader, at every level, from the senior leaders to the middle leaders – is able to turn the vision into actions. That cohesion is key, and without it it would be near impossible to make real change. As I moved further into the spring term, the school seemed to be in a place of limbo, where I'd often have conversations with a number of people who may or may not have recorded their lesson observations. Or who may or may not have fed back to the teachers whom they observed. Or who may or may not have misplaced a spreadsheet that had the breakdown of data on pupil progress from the previous term. So I may or may not be able to give you a sense of where we were. As you can imagine, not being able to have a clear overview of what was working and what wasn't was making it difficult to pinpoint where my focus needed to be. What I found particularly difficult on this journey was the lack of a sense of urgency with which the improvement of the academy needed to happen among the team.

Then one day I met with Peter Hughes, a fellow Future Leader. We had a long conversation about the joys of headship and some of the brick walls that I had come up against, whilst I explained my dilemma of having half a picture of what was going on in Crest. Peter introduced me to the holy grail of schooling: his platform called ProgressTeaching, which enabled him to map out and show me the most recent observations of all members of his teaching staff and the feedback that they were given. Not only did he have all of that information immediately at his fingertips, but he was also able to filter the information by term and department. For me, that was amazing. Finally, a tool that enabled me to read and get a sense of what the provision in the academy was like on a single screen. It was transformational. I took one look and didn't turn back.

The idea behind the quality of teaching and learning is a fairly complex one, but at its core it focuses on an essential leverage point: the quality of feedback. Like high-performing athletes, we have to make sure that the feedback we give as leaders is specific and very focused, and that people can act on it. Keen to utilise the vast knowledge that the leaders at Crest had, I set the expectation for all teachers to be entitled to at least one lesson observation per week, which in turn meant that staff members were entitled to at least one high-quality conversation around their practice per week. While on the surface this seemed like a slight tweak to what was already in place, it was a massive shift for staff from what teachers had historically experienced. We moved from three lessons observed per year to teachers having roughly 39 lesson observations. But it wasn't just about the number of observations. Research suggests that increasing observations itself doesn't lead to improvement in teaching but, instead, looking at what people have said and the quality of that feedback is fundamental and should then be used to feed into CPD.

It wasn't only the expectation of observations that needed to change; the mindset of staff members had to shift simultaneously. The aim was to move observations from compliance and quality-assurance to seeing feedback as a tool that was there to improve the overall quality of teaching. We moved away from leaders going into lessons and telling the teachers what they were not doing very well, to me insisting that leaders went into lessons to support the teachers. It was then my job to hold the middle and senior leaders to account and, in turn, facilitate conversations around what was and wasn't working in terms of giving feedback – and, if necessary, questioning why, after so many feedback sessions, some teachers were not improving. I set out with the aim of repurposing both middle and senior leaders to focus on improving the quality of teaching and learning as, fundamentally, it doesn't just belong to the teaching and learning team, but to every leader in the school.

At the beginning of rolling out the new perspective of teaching and learning, it was very interesting. I was honestly surprised at how little teaching and learning mattered to some leaders. The process of a culture shift is genuinely a massive one but, for me, arguably the most important factor in a child's learning is the quality of the teaching and learning that they receive. Teaching and learning is what matters and, essentially, that is it. In SLT briefings, I'd have the overview page of our dashboard displayed on a screen, outlining the total of observations that had been carried out by members of the team. I'd have people who carried out a significant number and, understandably, areas that were under their responsibility would be improving. And then I'd have other members of the team who didn't do as many observations, and in briefings we'd facilitate conversations around the reasons why their areas were not improving. This helped to vividly illustrate the fact that the more opportunities we gave staff to talk about teaching and learning, the more opportunities they had to improve their practice.

The school was inspected again by Ofsted within 19 months and was judged as good. Among a number of things that were highlighted in the report, I think the most fundamental aspect of improvement was our focus on CPD and teaching and learning. I was able to build a team of like-minded leaders who really embraced the idea that teaching and learning was an essential part of the leadership function and strategy.

The solution

People. Systems. Data. We've talked about the people, we've talked about the systematic approach, but we also need to talk about the data and the benefit of using it to plan CPD. It's important that we collect, collate and analyse the information on teaching and learning and the feedback that's been given and received. It is this information that allows us to plan CPD that aligns to teachers' needs. Too often, CPD is linked to the latest trend, which can be based on research rather than being driven by an analysis of observations and coaching sessions that your teachers have received. Using tangible information to understand what you are good at as an organisation and what needs to improve should always be the starting point. Without this data, you are at best guessing the school's strengths, areas for development and associated CPD requirements. We all think that we know our schools, but I recommend you read *Thinking, Fast and Slow* by Daniel Kahneman (2011). Heuristics can be a powerful force.

A similar situation exists within The Mossbourne Federation. As I've previously stated, I don't believe that retention is the panacea that people make it out to be; as such, the predominant model at Mossbourne is the up-or-out approach. The private sector has done this for years. Companies such as GE and Inditex seek to hire a large group of individuals at the entry level and train them to the highest level of competency and ability. This often leads to them being head-hunted by other organisations. I have a relentless, determined and non-flinching professional and personal commitment to making a positive difference in children's lives and to the community of educators. Therefore, our schools train teachers who join us to the highest quality. Within six years, half would have left, some for external promotions, others to go overseas, etc., but many remain, staying in the federation for the long term.

If I can keep ECTs for four to six years, that's great, and it doesn't preclude what I call my mainstays – those who have stayed with us and have acquired the institutional knowledge, which is invaluable. Two of my current heads have been with the federation or its predecessor school (the Newham school from where a significant number of the original Mossbourne staff came) since they were newly qualified teachers (now known as ECTs) for their entire career. Those with institutional knowledge are a gift, but some may also be blockers to change – but that's OK. You just need to be cognisant, particularly in turn-around schools, where you frequently hear people say, 'We've always done it this way.'

The final words

'Practice does not make perfect. Only perfect practice makes perfect.'
(Vince Lombardi)

My final thought here is that I would never judge a school, department or individual teacher by the aggregation of the specific elements of their practice. The aggregation of these elements merely highlights possible strengths and areas for development. The underlying qualitative information always provides a deeper and richer picture.

Teachers are not numbers; we need to know what they are good at, what they are working on and what other people have said to them. As well as this, it is important to know their aspirations and hopes, in order to help them to become the best teacher that they can be. Collect the quantitative data from observations and use it to point you in the right direction, but always read the underlining narrative. Be honest with your teachers: is their practice developing, effective or highly effective?

Top tips

- Use a research-based approach to teaching and learning. Avoid pseudoscience.
- Share the 'why' behind the research so that teachers implement it effectively.
- Create time in SLT to talk about teaching and learning weekly.
- Record all feedback given to teachers and use this information to plan CPD and assess the quality of teaching and learning in your school.
- Aggregation of the numbers is great for identifying strengths and areas for development, but remember that teachers are not numbers. Read the narrative.

7 Relationships

People work for people. The wonderful thing about education is that it has purpose built in. I don't need to explain our purpose; everyone understands the importance of what we do. In Chapter 2, I talked about the importance of the mission and the fundamental part that it plays in leading an exceptional school. In this chapter, I want to explore how the mission and purpose are underpinned by relationships. All schools have a purpose, many schools have a clear mission but not all of these schools are exceptional. The difference between a good school and a great school is the people. One can't have a relationship with everyone, but you can create a culture that places relationships at its heart.

The person who has the biggest influence on a student in school is their teacher; similarly, the person who has the biggest influence on your day-to-day life at work is your teacher (aka your line manager). Children work for their teachers and staff work for their line managers. Every time I speak to someone who is upset with their job, in any sector, normally the first thing that they say is that they don't like their boss. This is because people work for people. This chapter seeks to remind you of the intrinsic value of relationships and what they bring to our schools; it looks at the leadership skills of analysis and research, and focuses on motivation, culture and behaviour. I will also introduce you to Glen Denham from New Zealand, who talks about the importance of relationships with a particular focus on what we can learn about them from Māori culture. My final thoughts will revolve around two significant events that have influenced my journey.

The yarn

A few years ago, following the Year 11 mock GCSE examinations, I was asked to take over a class, and of course I said yes. The principal had made the difficult decision to replace the teacher, as the children were not realising their potential. It was clear that without immediate action, the children's GCSE maths grades would suffer significantly. The principal had been open and honest about their concerns with the teacher, because the children were and always have been our biggest priority – bigger than anyone's ego. The teacher was rightly devastated but the decision was made because our primary purpose is educating children. Of course, nobody wants to undermine staff in this way, but I repeat: our primary purpose is educating children. We can't and must never forget this.

As the CEO of a growing MAT, it goes without saying that I had a million things on my to-do list. But I've never said no to teaching an extra class ever (this wasn't going to be the first). Teaching is in my blood and is something that I absolutely love doing to this day. I can hear you. I can hear myself. 'It's not the leader's job to step in, do the task, get bogged down in the detail.' 'It's the leader's job to find a solution to the problem.' 'It's the leader job to lead.' For me, not doing the detail – not stepping in when needed – is a concept that I've never accepted or fully taken on as a leader. I feel that an understanding of the detail has always helped me to be a better leader, as it allows me to coach and mentor my team more effectively. Stepping in when needed, as a working-class lad, is just part of my DNA. This aspect of my nature affords me the intimate knowledge of what it is like to work in my federation and allows me to empathise with my staff. However, for clarity, it's important that I state that, as a leader, if you always need to step in, then something is going seriously wrong with your organisation. This was not the case in this instance. As leaders, we can't forget that it's our job to look at the bigger picture, provide direction, oversee the people and offer them corrections when they drift off course. This is impossible if you spend all day in the trenches and don't take opportunities to look up at what is happening from a different viewpoint.

Going back to the teacher from whom I took over, I want to emphasise that the teacher was not sacked. Their teaching was not inadequate. In fact, I used the planning that they already had in place and the teacher continued producing lesson plans for each lesson for several weeks. Their planning was excellent – better than mine in many ways. Their delivery had always been solid, and their level of subject knowledge was also excellent. So, after this moment of clarification, I know exactly what you are thinking. Why was there a need to replace the teacher if the planning and subject knowledge were excellent and their delivery was solid? And why were the children not achieving the expected outcomes?

To put it simply, the teacher was apathetic. It was as though caring would imply a deficiency – a weak spot or a shortcoming – and the children knew it. It was very evident that the teacher believed that the job was merely to plan great lessons and deliver them, but there was a crucial factor missing – something so vital and so fundamental, yet we struggle when trying to find the words to make it tangible. If you haven't watched the TED Talk by the great Rita Pierson called 'Every kid needs a champion' (n.d.), you should. She talks about the value and importance of relationships in the classroom with such eloquence and passion. What was the magical ingredient that I brought into the classroom that was missing from the previous teacher's practice? I cared.

Now I don't for a minute think that anyone I meet sees me as soft and cuddly – not by a long shot – but, as you've gathered, I do love to talk when it comes to maths, education and leadership (in that order). I get an immense intrinsic reward from challenging and coaching people into achieving their very best, whether it be an adult or a child. Therefore, in true Peter John Hughes fashion, I believed in them. I motivated them. I taught them really well. And, as a result, I ended up with a tribe of dedicated mathematicians. They would freely come to the space in my boardroom to study and request help with their homework. They would attend Saturday boosters with me and listen to me rant and remind them of how brilliant, talented and exceptional they were and how far they could go. It was a symbiotic relationship. They were working for me as much as I was working for them.

Being passive is not our default mode as human beings, or else we would have been born as a quokka or a sloth (no offense to these lovely creatures). It is in our nature to work, to endeavour, to want and to move in a direction of something that we desire and deem valuable. Children, especially those with many contributing factors that make them disadvantaged – the ones that should fail and fail hard, according to statistics – need someone to believe in them, to enable the seed of possibility and belief to grow. It wasn't easy and of course they tested me, especially because of my CEO title, but if they told me that they couldn't do something, I would call them out on it, tell them that I didn't believe them and help them to prove themselves wrong, through guidance and support.

The data doesn't lie. The principal made the right decision. The children went from 4s and 5s in their mocks to 6s and 7s in their GCSE mathematics exams. Four children smashed it out of the park and achieved a grade 8, and for one of these it was an increase in four grades – a 4 to an 8. The key factor in all this was that I showed that I cared. I was invested and I expected the same in return. Between them and me, we created a pact through my insistence and expectation of their effort and communication. If, for instance, homework wasn't submitted, it was considered an afront on me because my students, at any time, could ask for help and it would never be refused. They even sent me invites to meetings in my school diary to book my time using their school email addresses (of course), in order to go over any work about which they were confused. Essentially, the work that they did for themselves got them so far, but working for someone else who believed in them took them further. They may not have all liked me all of the time, but they all knew that I cared. I think that it's a universal truth: children are motivated to work for themselves and their teacher when there is a positive relationship. This may be pseudoscience, but I like it.

Just take a moment and think back to your youth and when you worked your hardest for a teacher. For me, three teachers instantly come to mind: Mr Bailey, Mr Traynor and Miss Shiller. Mr Bailey taught me physics at Young Technology High School in Years 11 and 12 (the UK equivalent of Years 12 and 13). He had a unique passion for the subject that radiated out of him. He sincerely wanted every one of his students to do well. Mr Bailey was the vice-principal and he taught only one class and I was in it. Our classroom was a short hop from his office. We would wait in anticipation for him to arrive, which he always did eventually – often with only a piece of chalk and a textbook, ready to teach physics off the top of his head, like it was nothing. He would come in and start by asking us where we had left off from our previous lesson, and then the magic would begin. Regardless of the topic – circular motion, simple harmonic motion, moments, the list goes on – he would explain the concepts, derive the formulae and provide the perfect examples, all from memory. He was brilliant. From where I sat as a student, he didn't appear to have planned his lessons – on paper, at least. Why was he so good? He had the factors that make a great teacher, according to research – great subject knowledge and quality instruction – as well as the elusive factors: he cared for his students and demanded excellence.

That's not to say that I wasn't lucky in having lots of amazing teachers, many of whom I had the joy of teaching beside, but Mr Bailey stood out. In my second, third and fourth years of teaching, I returned to Young Technology High School, the school where I finished my secondary education. It was interesting to go back to the place where I had such fond memories of my physics and maths lessons. I wasn't always the best behaved at school but all of the staff that were still there (remember, this is a small town and therefore staff turnover is low) were welcoming, helpful and forgiving.

Mr Traynor, my 4 Unit (the Oz version of A level further maths) Higher School Certificate maths teacher, was another practitioner with exceptional subject knowledge and brilliant instruction, who was just a tiny bit scary. Unlike Mr Bailey, his lessons were planned in absolute detail. He carried a book of examples and carefully selected textbook exercises. He would skilfully copy the exercise and the homework from his 'book' to ensure that all was exactly as it should be. Although he was a little scary and things had to be 'just so', it felt like he cared, knew me and never stopped expecting the best from me. I wasn't just another student; I was Peter.

I recall a seminal conversation that took place when he sat me down in his office after I failed several tests because I was not completing my homework. I wasn't always as diligent and ambitious as I am now. He was clear that I was capable of doing the course but if I was unwilling to do homework, I would fail. There were many contributing factors that made me a disadvantaged student, and some hurdles and habits are hard to battle and even harder to overcome. I'd never had the structure or routine throughout my life that promoted the importance of homework, but he wasn't going to lower the bar of expectations, even for 17-year-old me. Mr Traynor was delivering a hard truth, but my memory of this event is still a fond one. He was respectful, he was honest and he treated me as the young man that I was. He gave me an 'out', lifting the pressure from me to develop skills that didn't exist and that would continue to be a struggle for me, even at university. I dropped 4 Unit but continued to study 2 and 3 Unit maths, which he taught.

A huge part of leadership is knowing when to give people an out – a dignified out. The principal that I talked about earlier offered the maths teacher of my tribe an out in the same way as Mr Traynor offered me an opportunity to succeed, by structuring a difficult discussion in a way that didn't diminish my passion.

Mr Bailey and Mr Traynor were not the only ones looking out for me during my time at school. As I've said before, the written word has always felt insurmountable to me and is something with which I have struggled from a young age, due to my fragmented schooling and the challenges that I faced throughout my childhood. Ms Shiller, my English teacher, was yet another person who knew my history but didn't lower her expectations of me. I am eternally grateful for her support, guidance and patience. She gave me two gifts. One is an appreciation of 'The Road Not Taken' and other Robert Frost poems. The second was a gliding scholarship, which I achieved through Ms Shiller's help with writing my application essay. She knew that I wanted to be a pilot, and when I approached her to read my essay, she did so without hesitation.

Sometimes, people offer you something when they don't have to. For me, moving to the town Young was transformational. It's where the family that became my adopted family settled with me from the age of 15. It's where I met and was taught by amazing teachers that catapulted me into a position where I could and would become a teacher myself. It's the place where I was feeling safe enough (as a looked-after child who had found a forever home) to begin to grow roots. As you now know, through whispers of nuance or other yarns within this book, my life throughout my childhood and teens had been unconventional to say the least. I'd moved from location to location because of my parents' on-and-off relationship with each other and other spouses, giving me a fragmented notion of stability. I had collected cans from bins – up and down the main street and through back alleys – for money with my siblings, driven by my dad and his new wife, a memory that pains me still, to fund excursions that they had planned. I'd picked potatoes in the middle of winter between the age of six and eight, digging my hands into the frost-covered earth before the mist of the morning had lifted, to bring additional income into my family home. I've even eaten food that has been thrown out. Adverse experiences have a detrimental impact on a child's development and can eradicate hope, ambition and opportunities to achieve, but never underestimate the power of a champion. I had three champions in school as a teen when I needed them at this key point in my life.

Knowing what you now know, you can hopefully understand why, when Mr Bailey suggested to me one day that I put my hat in the ring to be school captain, I was shocked. But, due to his words, I did it anyway. In no way, shape or form did I expect to win. In all the places I'd lived, I had always been the poor kid, the smelly kid; it's how I saw myself too – as someone different and removed from my peers, in one way or another. Why would Mr Bailey encourage me, of all children, to put myself forward to be the school captain? Who knows? But he did and I still feel better for it today.

Sorry to burst your bubble, but I didn't win. This is a yarn and not a fairytale, after all, but I was elected to the position of prefect. I was elated. I would have never put myself forward of my own accord for anything that would have required an election if it had not been for Mr Bailey. Inside, a part of me will always be the little boy who needed to collect cans for money, but each day the label of 'disadvantaged' becomes less important and therefore less defining of who I am. Each time someone offers you something when they don't have to – whether that's belief, a nudge to enter a competition, an out, a quiet word – it makes a child (or adult, for that matter) stand a little taller and feel a little more valued, believed in and hopeful that maybe the impossible is possible, even if it's just for a moment. But isn't that just what life is about? Moments.

Mr Traynor continued to nurture; it was in his blood. When I worked alongside him after returning to Young Technology High School as a teacher, he continued to cultivate and encourage me. His encouragement and support were behind my successful application for my first leadership role as a year advisor (head of year in the UK). As you know, I disappeared off to the UK before starting my fifth year of teaching, but all of these relationships contained seminal moments for me. Whether these people know this or not, they have led me to where I am today.

Although not always tangible, never underestimate the power of connection. In her TED Talk, Rita says:

> *'you know your toughest kids are never absent... you won't like them all, and the tough ones show up for a reason... It's the relationships... Every child deserves a champion, an adult who will never give up on them, who understands the power of connection, and insists that they become the best that they can possibly be...'*

Although this yarn mainly focuses on teachers who were my champions, I could just as easily have waxed lyrical about leaders who have also played this same role and become my champions when I needed them in my career. It's just as important for a leader to champion their staff as it is for a teacher to champion their students.

Leadership skills

Analysis: Detailed examination of anything in order to understand it

Great school culture allows great moments to happen. There are powerful moments where teachers influenced my life, but how do we as leaders create an environment where these moments happen for our children and our staff? In this section, I will analyse how we can use the study of business culture to deliberately think about and create culture in a school environment.

Often, when we talk about culture in schools, we give simple sound bites like 'sweat the small stuff', 'inclusive', 'no excuses', 'children come first'... The list is endless. All of these sound bites are useful in describing elements of a school's culture but fall short of providing the full picture. For example, how do staff interact with each other in a 'Children come first' culture? Such sound bites provide little help in assessing a school's culture and even less help in understanding how to move or transform it. We as leaders must be able to reflect on our culture, assess it and know which levers to pull to move our culture in the desired direction.

If company culture is defined as 'the way we do things round here' then, in simple terms, a company's culture, or a school's culture for that matter, is the sum of all its interactions. Therefore, any model that looks at culture must have relationships at its heart. Goffee and Jones (1996) place relationships at the centre of culture when they describe it as 'community' – a definition that fits well in many environments, but particularly that of a school. I feel that there is strong synergy here between business and school culture because they look at community through the lens of sociology, which breaks relationships into two types: sociability (friendship) and solidarity (pursuit of shared objectives). For Goffee and Jones, this use of sociology to look at culture helped to form their basis for examining and exploring four distinct types of culture:

- **Fragmented:** A community with low sociability and low solidarity is characterised by a lack of collaboration between the members. Individuals are focused on personal or professional objectives rather than organisational ones.

- **Networked:** A community high on sociability and low on solidarity is characterised by strong bonds and affiliation among its members, often socialising outside of work. The bonds between members of this community can take priority over organisational objectives.

- **Mercenary:** A community low on sociability and high on solidarity is characterised by its members' laser-like focus on achieving the organisational objectives. Members of this community often form short-term bonds focused around the task at hand.

- **Communal:** A community with high sociability and high solidarity is characterised by a sense of belonging, collaborative working and socialisation between members.

This is outlined in Goffee and Jones's (1996) 'two dimensions, four cultures' grid (see Figure 7).

I am going to draw upon some of my own experiences to help to demonstrate how the four cultures manifest in a school. As I walk you through, you may be able to make some comparisons with a range of school settings. You will come to understand that different parts of an organisation can operate simultaneously in different corners of the matrix. For example, you might find a communal maths department in a fragmented school. Is this good or bad? That's up to you to decide and think about. You need to decide which culture is right for your school. I am, of course, entitled to my own opinion and, for me, some cultures just don't work for schools.

I've worked in **fragmented** schools – if you haven't, then you are lucky. You can recognise these environments quite quickly, whether you are in one or simply passing through. They are the schools where the door is pulled shut. The environments where it's every person for themselves. I've experienced this mainly in failing schools in which I have previously worked and from listening to stories of leaders who have been parachuted into schools to 'turn them around'.

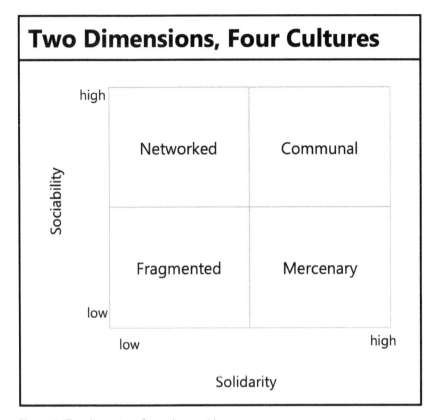

Two Dimensions, Four Cultures

high
Sociability

Networked | Communal

Fragmented | Mercenary

low

low | high

Solidarity

Figure 7 *Two dimensions, four cultures grid*

When I look back now at my first experience of working in a failing school, there was low sociability and low solidarity. I remember it like it was yesterday, I walked into the staffroom and no one said 'Hello'. I was brand new to the UK (having landed at Gatwick Airport but 30 hours ago) and to the school. I put my bag down in the corner of the room and I sat alone, waiting to be directed to the class in which I would be working in order to start my day. After some time, a person finally appeared to take me to my next destination. I naturally went to follow the staff member, leaving my backpack where it lay in the staffroom. They stopped me, pointed at my belongings and said, 'I wouldn't leave that there.' With this one comment, I quickly learned that, in this environment, the staff stole from each other.

I was only meant to be at the school for a day, but the principal offered me a contract on the spot and told me that if I stayed they would pay me more money. He offered no inspirational speech, no motivating mantra, no greater purpose to stay, other than an increased daily long-term supply rate. I must say at 25 per cent it was a generous increase. It wasn't about the children (on the surface) – he didn't give me a narrative or tell me about the journey that the school was on – he just offered me money to stay. I'm not saying that this was the wrong approach at all. With the wisdom I now have, I understand that it's hard – well, actually impossible – to build solid foundations on quicksand. A principal needs good people to stay and work with them if they are going to create a good school and give children the holistic education that they need and deserve.

I worked in a school with a **networked** culture when I moved 1,000 km away from Sydney to a place called Bourke to start my first year of teaching. In the state of New South Wales, newly qualified teachers were put into a teaching pool, a process in which a teacher would apply to the state (and not individual schools) and then be deployed like army folk across the area. If you were a 'gold star recruit', you were guaranteed a job; the rest were put on a list and had to wait for their number to be drawn. Those on the list went where they were told. I was on the list – no gold star for me.

Bourke is one of the places where no one wants to go. You are expected to do three years there, after which you are rewarded with a priority transfer that gets you sent back to the beautiful coast to work out the rest of your career. The main reason why no one wanted to go to Bourke as a young newly qualified teacher was because it was a small town of less than 3,000 people in the middle of nowhere. There was nothing exciting to do at all. Once you were there, you had no choice but to be sociable. On a Friday night, *the whole school* would decant to the pub and sit out in the beer garden under the shade – it was Oz, after all – and bond. The pub would also give us teachers and support staff free food to sweeten the deal. As a group of young people new to town, in a small school, and 150 km west from, well, anywhere, your only option on a Friday night was to have a drink or ten with your fellow colleagues – that and to build a really strong relationship with the deputy talking about rugby. One Thursday night, a group of us 22-year-old teachers were presented with some fantastic news. A new maths teacher had arrived a few months into the academic year. This was a big event, so we dragged the new arrival out to North Bourke (an area five minutes' drive away and consisting of a pub and petrol station) and partook of the delights of the North Bourke Hotel while playing darts. After emerging from home the next morning, feeling a little worse for wear, I went into work and headed straight to my pigeon hole – the place from which to collect messages before emails existed. What I found was a merit certificate from my principal, which said: 'Thanks for showing Henry the delights of North Bourke.'

The principal knew that a social culture was important; he needed high sociability, so that us young pups didn't get homesick and leave before our allocated time. It was a networked community and it worked. We did what we needed to do to teach well. We had a purpose, but it leaned more towards the staff than the children. The sociability was all about the staff; it was essential, as it enabled the principal to combat the mobility of teachers. The principal was ensuring that the children in his community had a great education. I could imagine that, at the extreme end, if we had all stayed for longer than three years and chosen to live in the town, it would have been very possible for the school to become outstanding, as this culture would have moved towards a communal one.

I also worked in a school with a **mercenary** culture, where pupil outcomes were the driving force for everything. In fact, it was my school in my first years of headship. I was definitely a mercenary leader. Teachers who were not delivering for children would be shown the door and people would think nothing of it. They would think that it was fair. Staff knew that the only focus was exceptional outcomes for children. It was this singular focus that allowed Mossbourne to thrive in an environment where children had been failed for so long. Sometimes, doing what is right and not what is popular is essential to give children what they deserve. Yet what I recognised is that this singular focus doesn't allow for the innovation and reimagining that is required to stay at the top – but it will get you there.

There are many other situations in schools where a mercenary culture works. Take the example of safeguarding. I know that I want my safeguarding team to be focused on a singular objective: the safeguarding of our children. I want my designated safeguarding lead to lead with clarity and precision, so that there can be no ambiguity about what is expected. When a member of staff doesn't follow the protocol, I would expect them to be reminded and have their actions corrected immediately. Anything else has the potential to put children at greater risk.

I have also worked in a school with a **communal** culture. I'd like to think that this is where our federation and schools are now. For me, a communal culture is the right one for a high-performing school. This doesn't mean that this culture is a requirement. As you've read, mercenary will get you there. There are also schools that I have visited that are clearly networked, achieving success and doing great things for children. However, it is the unique blend in communal that I feel puts a school in a place to sustain the exceptional outcomes for pupils. For us, it's having the absolute clarity of a mercenary purpose (changing children's lives for the better by creating an environment where learning is the norm) and its resulting artefacts, mixed with the networked sense of belonging and collaborative working, where staff do go above and beyond, that has established us as being exceptional.

Research: The collecting of information about a particular subject

Relationships are critical because you can't start anything without them or without good people. It is the fuel that starts things, but it can only get you so far. To move further, you then need to create processes and systems that help you to get to the next step. These are then underpinned by great knowledge, data and information, which helps inform leaders to make great decisions. In this section, the focus is on research that reinforces the importance of recognising that the development of culture is a strategic art with a touch of science.

In the previous piece of analysis, we looked at culture through the lens of sociology, as a community and its relationships. This model is very good at allowing us to identify the culture in our schools through a two-dimensional framework. However, it only provides us with two levers to pull in order to improve school culture. For example, I can quickly identify that my failing school is fragmented and therefore know that I need to create a common sense of purpose. Or I can identify that my science department is not producing great outcomes because the staff are not challenging each other professionally, as they are all too friendly and in a networked culture. It is a great model with which to identify a problem, as it helps you to assess where you are and possibly where you want to be, but it has its limitations when it comes to changing and developing a culture.

However, as far back as 1997, Pascale, Milleman and Gioja, in 'Changing the way we change', identified four distinct levers that I believe work well alongside the aforementioned two-dimensional framework. These levers are invaluable when thinking about shifting culture. The article offers us four elements that can be used to bring about substantial cultural change:

- **Identity:** The sense of belonging – do staff identify with the school?
- **Power:** The ability to affect change – do employees feel that they have the power to make a difference?
- **Conflict:** How problems are solved – are conflicts resolved quickly and in the best interests of the school?

- **Learning:** How new ideas are received – is the school open to hearing and trying new ideas?

Changing a culture takes time and involves honest, open communication at all levels. One of the standout quotes for me from the article is one that identifies the need to adjust a leader's mindset, because it reminds us to think about motivation and how it presents in the workplace. Pascale et al. (1997) ask the reader to 'see employees as volunteers who decide each day whether or not to contribute the extra ounce of discretionary energy that will make the difference'. Cultural change involves bringing people together in small groups that can feed into bigger discussions in order to look at issues and find solutions. Engaging staff and seeing them as meaningful contributors is motivating and empowering. This way of cascading the involvement of all staff is a great way to engage individuals. But bringing people together is the hard part, of course. You may have disillusioned individuals or naysayers. You may have individuals who are not confident about speaking up initially, but cultural change does not happen if you do nothing. It is what makes it a deliberate act for highly successful leaders.

Identity can be a difficult one in education to capture. There is a natural inclination for teachers to associate with both their profession and also with their school. At my federation, we refer to our children as Mossbournians and the same could be said for staff. What features drive identity? Identity is developed through celebrating success and gathering people together for a shared purpose. We often say of our most dedicated staff that if you cut them down the middle you would see the word 'Mossbourne' written through them. School songs, federation conferences, stories, etc. bring us together and give us a sense of belonging.

Power needs to be disturbed and delegated. There still needs to be the final decision-maker. However, that doesn't mean that others are not needed to influence and contribute to solving the challenging needs of a school. I've always seen huge benefits in a flat management structure, with its goal to have as little hierarchy as possible. It elevates the level of responsibility and communication because it creates fewer levels of management.

Conflict and its resolutions are often the hardest skills for a leader to learn and develop. Critical conversations and knowing how to react when someone is disagreeing with you are things that you need to practise, and you can't practise if you are conflict-averse. Are your meetings quiet? If they are, promote discussion and create spaces where professional discourse can take place. It's OK to agree to disagree. Safe spaces need to be created by leaders, as this is where new ideas can be formulated.

Learning – we have so much to learn from one another, so much that each of us can bring to the table. For me, I entrust most of the biggest tasks to the practitioners themselves, as they are great opportunities for growth. For instance, my teaching and learning teams, made up of the leads from each school, were the ones who developed, designed and disseminated a new rubric to evaluate teaching and learning across the federation. It makes absolute sense to encourage and support this team to do this, rather than impose views from above, with a complete disregard to what is happening day in, day out in classrooms. It's vital to be open to learning from others, and this also includes using consultations and focus groups with the staff. However, we must be careful to remain agile and avoid death by consultation – we've all been there.

In conclusion, relationships are indeed critical to the success of any organisation, including schools. However, creating and maintaining a positive culture also requires a deliberate, strategic effort that involves developing identity, power, conflict-resolution skills and a commitment to continuous learning. By leveraging the insights of Pascale et al. (1997), schools can move beyond the limitations of a two-dimensional framework for assessing culture and take a more holistic approach that considers the four distinct levers of culture. This approach involves bringing people together, creating safe spaces for discourse and empowering staff to contribute to the school's success. By doing so, school leaders can create a communal culture that fosters innovation, collaboration and continuous improvement, ultimately resulting in improved outcomes for students.

Case study: Glen Denham, Principal (secondary), New Zealand

Introduction

My friend Glen Denham has had a very successful life. He played for the New Zealand basketball team in Sydney 2000 Olympic Games before I met him on the Future Leaders programme. He subsequently went on to move a school in Croydon, England, from inadequate to outstanding. After Denham spent

15 years working at schools in the United Kingdom, he returned to New Zealand as principal of Massey High School and, in 2022, he was appointed headteacher of Wellington College.

Case study

'He tangata, he tangata, he tangata.' ('It is people, it is people, it is people.' – Māori saying when asked the question, 'What is the most important thing in life?')

I am a New Zealander of Māori descent. My *iwi* (tribal) affiliation is Ngati Rangitihi and the *waka* (canoe) that brought my tribe to Aotearoa (Māori name for New Zealand) is Te Arawa. I am proud to be Māori. Over the last 20 years, I have been blessed to lead schools in the UK and in New Zealand. All but my current school have been in areas of great deprivation and poverty. I have also been fortunate to have played basketball for New Zealand for 16 years, and 13 of those years as the captain.

When I was little, my dad, who was heavily involved in the trade unions, introduced us to his friend. He was a union leader and a giant of a man, and he worked at the local freezing works. I was mesmerised by his hands. He had the word 'hate' tattooed on his right-hand set of knuckles and 'love' tattooed on his left-hand set of knuckles. I looked at his hands and thought that the love hand must be for shaking hands with people and the hate hand must be for hitting people with. What happens if he gets his hands mixed up? I thought that if he only had 'love' tattooed on both hands, no one would be afraid of him. In actuality, everyone did love him and he gave that love right back. Years later, I asked him why he didn't get the hate tattoo removed. He rolled up both sleeves and on the underside of his right wrist he had the word 'under' tattooed, and on the underside of his left wrist he had the word 'standing'. He held out his hands palm down to me. He said, 'I used to be a brawler, a fighter and then I took this work on. Leading people, taking care of people and helping people. [He turned his hands palm up] Its only in understanding others that we can truly help them and love them. [He rotated his hands, turning them over and over and over.] Hate drives you under and love is the best place to be standing.' He put his massive hands on my shoulders and said, 'Son, always lead with love.'

If you had to have two words tattooed or etched on your leadership heart – two words that your leadership soul rested on, two words that when people spoke about you always came up – what would they be? For me, it would be 'love' and 'faith' – to love who you serve and to have faith in where you are taking your people to. Both love and faith are only possible with authentic, transparent, meaningful relationships. Embracing and sharing our vulnerabilities. In fact, mountains can be moved when you tell someone that you love them and have faith in them. It turns people into champions. If you close your eyes right now, I know that you can see all of those people that love you and have faith in you and are a big part of the reason why you are reading this book. Hold on to that love, ball it up into a neverending stream of energy and give it out in all your interactions to all you meet.

In the Māori culture, I lean on three core tenets that have held me and everyone I ever led in good stead and kept us all in great heart. The first is *manaakitanga*. It is the nurturing of relationships, looking after people and being very careful about how others are treated. It's at the core of our culture. No one should leave conversations with us with their dignity or respect not intact. I have had many conversations where I am holding people to account – more than I can remember. Sometimes I have had to let staff go (as my mum said, 'employ in haste, repent at leisure'), and I have been on a number of disciplinary panels where I have had to tell parents that their child is excluded from school. None of this is enjoyable but it's our job. What we can control is the tone, the empathy, the listening in these conversations. *Manaakitanga* is the holding of another person's dignity and treating it with the utmost respect.

Whanaungatanga is a relationship created through shared experiences and working together. It provides people with a shared sense of belonging. There is a brilliant activity in which all SLTs that I have led have participated. You ask them all to bring one thing – a photo or a memento. In *whanaungatanga* sessions in which I have participated, people have brought a button, a report card, their old school blazer and a rejection letter from a job that they applied for. There are no rules around what people bring. You get each person to stand up and speak about what their item means, why it's important to them and why it relates to why they are here and on this team. It is usually very emotional and there are always tears, but we always leave with greater understanding of each other and know 'why' people are here. We also always leave much closer as a team. Without doubt, it is an incredibly humbling and binding experience.

The last value and, I believe, the most important is *whakaiti*. It means humility. The leader does not take credit for work but empowers others. There is no self-promotion. Humility means that great leadership is behind the scenes. My job as the headteacher is to provide shade and shelter. When things are going brilliantly and people are singing our praises, you will never find me. I am in the shade, making sure that others are in the sunshine. When things are going poorly and there is trouble, you will only ever find me. I provide the shelter for everyone else.

I am blessed to call the author of this book my friend and my brother. I have learned lots from him and other incredible leaders. Go and find your leadership tribe – your leadership *whanau* (family). Those that will nourish you and challenge you and make you think. Compassion over anger, empathy over judgement and listening over talking. I am by no means perfect. I think that I will be unfinished until the day I die. I think that being unfinished and still working on our best selves, our best human being, until we draw our last breath is a good way to be.

Arohanui, Glen

The solution

People, systems and data. People work for people. Understanding people, valuing them and giving them opportunities is the key. The way in which you build relationships is through asking questions, finding out what a person's capacity is and working with them. It enables you to develop them and their skills. Listen to people, be aware of how they are feeling, think about how to get the best out of them, be aware of the external demands that they have and be honest with them but never rude or belittling. You won't lower your expectations, but you can adapt and find ways in which to work with them, ensuring that they are fulfilling their purpose while still improving outcomes for children.

On a day-by-day basis, people work with their direct line manager. They are responsible for the development of their teams as much as the senior leaders in schools. Coaching, mentoring and communication with this key group needs to be factored in regularly in many organisations, but especially in schools. A lot of staff put a lot of effort into optional work. There are no shortcuts and we need people who will go the extra mile. Schools don't work if everyone is doing the bare minimum and if there is no element of goodwill. It's a fact.

People don't want to disappoint, and this truth lives everywhere around great schools that have a great culture. From the staff working front of house in the main office, to the deputies normally coordinating multiple tasks at any given time, to the children in their lessons, to the site team with the neverending list of tasks. Most people have an inherent desire to belong and be an important part of something greater than themselves. We all work harder for people who are invested in us. Many people talk about the impact of relationships but do not unpick the nuances of why this ingredient is particularly salient in schools.

The final words

A school is the principal's personality. Being a CEO is a lonely job; we are 'people people', after all.

We need to think about relationships when forming organisations and teams. There are two major events that I recollect as I conclude this chapter on relationships (and leadership). The first event occurred in my second year of teaching in Young. I'd been redeployed to my home town after a single year in Bourke. It wouldn't be long before I'd be working alongside the teachers who had taught me. One afternoon, after the regular pastoral leaders' meeting, the principal pulled me aside to give me some career advice and tell me that she thought I had the potential to be a principal one day. This blew me away. Still in the early years of my teaching career, I was in that phase of struggling to get all my books marked on time and as quickly as possible, so that I could go home and go out with my mates. I had no words to formulate a coherent response, but she saw something in me that I, at the time, didn't.

The second event happened the following year, when my head of department pulled me aside and said, 'I don't think that you are performing at your best. You are working at 80 per cent of your capability, but that's still better than the majority of the department.' I was stunned. He had called me out and he was right to. I was coasting. The thing here is that he did not need to come and talk to me; my teaching was good. As he said, I was outperforming many of my colleagues, with very little effort (how conceited do I sound?). Yet his awareness as a leader and his ability to see something in me became a huge mechanism for me to change in my career. It triggered my working-class values and lit a fire.

Some people need to be challenged to do their best. Both leaders chose to have these conversations with me. They saw something in me back then and planted a seed of belief. As leaders, we need to recognise the power of words; they can be used to nurture, slap people down or bring people on a journey, so they need to be used carefully and with thought.

Lastly, I want to tell you about Rob. I adored him. I've said that we all work for people but, in some cases, we learn just as much if not more from line-managing others – or maybe I should call it what it was in this case: being up-managed. I was assigned to manage the maths department with the hugely experienced Rob Walker, who was the head of department and who had achieved the highest Key Stage 3 SATs maths results in the country. I was a trainee senior leader who knew nothing. Here I was, being asked to line-manage one of the *best heads of maths in the country* (yes, I repeat), who also happened to be old enough to be my dad. I very quickly learned that he could have easily been a senior leader anywhere, due to his level of experience, knowledge and skills. He just chose not to be. I also learned very quickly that Rob Walker did not start work until the second period at 10.00 am, every day, and that was that: flexibility at its best.

It was a daunting task. Who was I to line-manage this person, who had more experience and knowledge of teaching maths in their little finger than I did in my entire being? Yes, he was old school and would shout at children, but yes, there would also be streams of students lining up at lunch and breaktime outside his office door, to show him their exercise books. He would see how much work they had done, he would check their understanding by asking them to explain a problem and then send them on their way. Unorthodox? You can decide for yourself, but he showed them that he cared, that their teachers cared and that he was invested.

At no time during our 'line manger' meetings did he ever belittle me, undermine me – when he very easily could have – or be dismissive due to my lack of leadership experience. Did he recognise potential or did he take pity on me? I'll never know, yet what I'm sure of is that if I asked him to do something, he would do it – but not before he offered challenge and critique, in a playful way, to coach and mentor but never to undermine. I loved this man dearly up until the day he died and beyond.

We have a plaque above his classroom door and an award named after him: the Rob Walker Prize for Excellence. It is awarded annually to the student who achieves the highest average point score across all of their GCSE subjects.

The key thing here is what I always say to students when I present them personally with the Rob Walker Prize at the Year 11 ball, dressed to the nines in my tux: 'If you ever sat in a maths lesson and wondered why so many children in Mossbourne love maths, the answer is Rob Walker.' Relationships matter.

Top tips

- Never underestimate the power of relationships.
- People work for people.
- Great systems allow great people to be greater by freeing up cognitive load.
- Information informs exceptional practice.

A floating elephant

Well done! You've found the final one.

This is the last of the elephants, but by no means the least important. There are often aspects of the role and school life that are not spoken about with flair because, quite simply, they are considered the 'boring stuff'. It's the magic that we all know about, but it doesn't make the headlines. The magic that can go unnoticed until it is no longer present and the wheels start falling off a well-oiled machine. I guess that It's why I've made it an elephant to draw your attention to it and remind you that the day-to-day aspects of the job really are important but don't always get the recognition. The magic is found in those moments when you say to yourself, 'I've done nothing today' when really you've done everything that was needed and more. This elephant has learned to float and learned to tread water and make it seem effortless. Never underestimate what a tremendous skill this is.

I had my vice-principal Veronica Carol as my rock – my critical friend – but she was also known as the mother of Mossbourne. Veronica was a maths teacher, who gave of herself to others. She provided clarity that allowed excellence to thrive, and everyone respected her. Veronica's influential but subtle presence commanded it. She would tell you when you went wrong, but she was also the person whom you went to when you made a mistake or needed help and advice. She, to me, represented excellence, no excuses and unity. When she opened the school with its founding principal, heels were not allowed. On the first day, as the children were welcomed in through the gates, she noticed that one child (whose parent was a local authority employee) came in with a tiny heel on her shoes. The principal wanted to let her go but Veronica pulled him aside and said, 'If you let that go, you will be allowing heels forever.' She held us all to account – even Sir Michael.

Her view was that you either change the rule or you follow it. She knew that the rules were there for a reason and that's what excellence is about. No shortcuts. It was on this basis that she was the key person to support me in the design of our new school. Her level of detail was superb. Her thinking pathways and perspectives were invaluable. Passive supervision, spaces where children could discuss issues with staff, safe places where pupils could wait for teachers outside of the classrooms, safety in the toilet areas – she dissected it all and put it back together to create a space that would change children's lives for the better, by creating an environment where learning is the norm.

She held the line to ensure that teachers maintained the standard for pastoral care and academic expectations. She wouldn't accept excuses. She would find a way to make things happen. Veronica didn't shy away from the difficult conversations in parent meetings. She was honest. She was open. She was direct. These are attributes that you need when raising expectations and instilling self-belief in children and their parents, who hadn't always been treated well. Veronica wasn't afraid to remind staff of their duties: the obligation to turn up on time for break duty, to support homework clubs and to go the extra mile for the pupils under our charge. She wouldn't allow poverty or deprivation to put a ceiling on things for our children. She was the consistent, unwavering magic of Mossbourne, and people didn't want to disappoint her.

There is a great safety in routine for children. It is especially important for those who arrive at the school gates every day on time, in a neat uniform that disguises the chaos that they may have just left behind. Students knowing the expectations and that the school will be the same every day, where key events are planned in the school year and knowing that key adults are always available to them, is the thing that can change pupils' lives for the better. If someone is upset when you set a boundary, it's a good sign, as it means that it was needed. We prioritise the needs over the wants, because our children deserve the best. Creating a consistent, safe, trusting school for children and staff does not happen without the Veronicas of the world.

8 Big shoes to fill

Some leaders have big personalities, some have reached heights never touched before and some have led quietly with a steadfast mission. When we move into a role, our focus is often on stepping into the metaphorical big shoes that need to be filled, but in reality it is much, much bigger than that. The big shoes that really need to be filled are those of the role and not those of the previous principal. These shoes already found their owner – you – the moment that you answered the call and accepted the job. This chapter focuses on my journey to finding my shoes and the reality of how I became the CEO of one of the top-performing MATs in the country. I use the skills of exploration and background to focus on my first year as principal, the codification of the federation and our values. I do this in order for people to understand that the path is not always straightforward. Dr Timothy Wiens, a principal, an academic and an inspirational leader in the USA, is the focus for this chapter's case study, where he shares his view on the responsibility that we hold as educational leaders. My final thoughts build on those of Wiens, where I reflect further on the levels of accountability that come with our roles.

The yarn

This is my CV from the moment I landed in the UK:

School 1 (2 years)	School 2 (4 years)	School 3 (Mossbourne)
☐ Maths teacher	☐ Deputy Head of Maths	☐ Future leaders SLT placement
■ Head of Year	☐ Advanced Skill Teacher	■ Deputy Principal
☐ Deputy Head of Year	☐ Acting SLT role	☐ Co-Acting Principal
☐ 2nd in Department and Numeracy Co-Ordinator	■ Future Leaders Programme (1st time)	☐ Principal (plus new school build)
	☐ Future Leaders Programme (2nd time)	☐ Executive Principal
		☐ CEO

Key

■ Unsuccessful ☐ Successful

Additional achievements

- Executive MBA from Oxford Saïd Business School
- ProgressTeaching Founder and CEO

I share the timeline of my career because having a chapter titled 'big shoes to fill' really has to start by retelling and remembering my own career journey. It has been an adventurous one, one on which I have been fortunate to be guided – sometimes without even knowing that it was happening. To those who demonstrated kindness and passed on their wisdom, I am forever grateful. I think a lot about the people who inspired me or encouraged me to believe in myself, especially during the period of writing this book.

Even if the unwanted phantom of imposter syndrome sits lurking in the background, when you contemplate the next step in your career, don't stop. Remember Katie Bedborough's 60 per cent rule. In my experience, people don't start a role when they are 100 per cent ready – then move on from it to the next challenge. A part of you must believe that you can do it – whatever the 'it' might be at the time. Applying for year group lead, science subject coordinator, children's centre principal… it's important to take the leap. Be afraid but do it anyway. It's also true that you need people to guide you to this place of believing when you are blinded to it yourself. There are some wonderful people in this world who find you when you are not even looking for them.

My physics teacher when I was 16 was one of them. Mr Bailey encouraged me to put myself forward for the role of school captain. My maths teacher, Mr Traynor, was another. He was extremely strict but careering. He told me that if I wanted to do 4 Unit maths (equivalent to further maths), I needed to do my homework. My English teacher, Ms Shiller, relentlessly worked her socks off to help me. As I had no knowledge on which to draw, she helped me to piece together enough understanding of the English language to keep moving forwards. Imagine if she knew that I'd written a book. These people set you on a path that you don't even see at the time. You may not even realise that they are helping you to form your own narrative, which you will need on your journey at a future point. People had belief when I didn't even imagine that the things that I have achieved were possible.

You may sit here reading this thinking that I was a boy destined to come out the other side, but as the Australian Aboriginal proverb says, 'Traveller, there are no paths. Paths are made by walking.' We often believe that we can plan every part of our lives. The reality is that whichever path you are walking on now is the path on which you are meant to be. The possibilities in front of you and the choice that you make to engage with them (or not) define you and, ultimately, your journey. Yes, I'm highlighting some of the positives, but the knockbacks quite often offer the most poignant lessons. It's important to take risks: sometimes you fail and sometimes you succeed, but both teach valuable lessons and are important.

When I'd applied for an acting senior leadership role, after being in my second London school for three years, I came into the school as a deputy head of maths and had gone on to be promoted to an AST. I'd seen the vacancy advertised and approached the principal to inquire whether they were open to taking an application from me. I have always believed that one should have a conversation before applying for an internal role. Be open to a positive or negative response and be willing to give both as a leader. I filled out the form and submitted my paperwork for the vacancy. Four people applied. Three got called to interview; I was not one of them. No one discussed it with me, no one gave me feedback and it hurt. It was at that point that I decided that I needed to put up or shut up. I realised that I needed to do things properly, so I got my pen back out again and applied to the Future Leaders programme. And guess what? They didn't think that I had the potential to be a leader (the first time round) either. My application was declined.

A year later, I reapplied for the Future Leaders programme, knowing that following the completion of the programme I would have to give the providers a third of my increase in salary for two years, e.g. if my salary was £40k before the programme and I was employed as a senior leader on £49k following the programme, they would take £6k (£3k pa). In addition, I would have to leave my current job to move into a senior leader's position at another school (on the same salary), with no guarantee of a job after the first year. This time I passed the assessment days and was sent to be interviewed by Sir Michael for a placement at his school. He offered me the role. Why? I was a great maths teacher, that's it. Well, that and I was cheap labour, because the programme covered a third of my salary. I'd like to say that I worked harder prior to my new application, but I didn't. I was still a young pup and in 'living my best life' mode.

Now I'm going to pause for a second and loop this back to some familiar themes: risk. Let's talk about why I ended up in the 'put up or shut up' position back at school two, when I was turned down for the acting SLT position. As previously mentioned, I'd been at the school for three years. I was becoming frustrated with the leadership and had started to think about how I would do it differently. The catalyst for this unease came from a significant moment that occurred when I was returning from a morning conference and walking down the hill back to the school. I saw two children in Year 11, sitting 50 metres outside the school gates, blatantly smoking a spliff. Of course, I went over and told them to stop and come with me. Safeguarding, behaviour policy, duty of care – alarm bells were obviously going off in my head. I kept insisting that they come with me, but they refused. So I went, as any diligent teacher would, to find a senior leader. The first one I found was the principal – fantastic, I thought. They were quickly joined by the deputy – even better. Perfect, I hear you cry. It was now just before lunch; I was worried about these boys and thinking about the next steps, as we obviously needed to do something. How do you think the leadership team responded? I'll be kind and not leave you speculating about the outcome. The decision was made to write a letter to the parents, telling them to talk to their children about the danger of drugs and recommending counselling. No sense of urgency to check on the children's immediate safety, no referrals, no follow-ups, no calls home and no checking that they had even returned to school. That was it – a letter. Yes, I challenged both the principal and the deputy about their decision and their duty to safeguard. And yes, this was not long before I applied for the acting SLT role.

I knew that if I ever became a senior leader, I wanted to be a good one, even if it took me two Future Leader applications to get there. It wasn't ever about being a principal for me – I just wanted to be a senior leader in order to prevent situations like this and others happening to children. So, let's bring the yarn back to my Future Leaders placement. I was coming to the end of my year and time at the school and a vice-principal job came up. Elation. I got my pen out again and applied for the vacancy. Did I get the job? I'll give you two guesses. Well, the answer is a big fat 'no'! I now found myself in a bind: I liked the school but there were no jobs there for me. The only logical solution was to start looking at other schools for a job, but the school felt like home and I wanted to stay. It hurt, but it was where I found myself and I had to accept it. In the calmness of reaching acceptance, I remembered something: that I was still an amazing maths teacher, and even the principal could not overlook this fact. I spoke to the principal and he offered me a role as a teacher of maths, with some additional responsibilities for me to take on. I was given what many considered in the school to be a poisoned chalice: the school timetable. All I saw was a wonderful puzzle to solve.

For the benefit of those who have never experienced the torment of organising and producing a secondary school timetable, it is an absolutely awful (wonderful) task. It is a task that people dread, due to the intricacies of it and the negative impact that it can have on the whole teaching staff body if you get it wrong. It causes people pain, sleepless nights, stress, tears and worry to such an extent that I'm sure some people are triggered just at the sheer mention of it. However, my brain loves problem-solving. For this reason, a task that many a secondary senior leader dreaded I took on with glee. As a result, it was the first time in the school's history that the timetable was completed in good time with minimal fuss. No shouting teachers, no children in the wrong places at the wrong time and no sleepless nights. It was done with no issues, and everyone was happy (as happy as they can be). To make it work, I asked the principal whether I could come to one of the SLT meetings to talk it through before the launch, because I needed to finalise some parts of the matrix. Historically, this had always been an SLT task, and I was not a senior leader anymore – my Future Leaders placement was over. I had come back in the September of the new academic year in the new role. I was a teacher with additional responsibilities now; therefore, in order to ensure that I had all of the information needed, I had to speak to the senior leaders for their input. The principal said yes to my request to join one SLT meeting, but what I didn't expect was that he would invite me to attend them all. This step, which was one of many, ended up being an unparalleled, unexpected career-changing opportunity for me to learn from leaders who were experts in their field.

The pursuit to achieve a title was, for me, the wrong approach; it was when I embraced the journey that my career flourished and prepared me for the job that I have now. **Remember: 'Traveller, there are no paths. Paths are made by walking.'** To be a good teacher (in all senses of the word), you must inspire others. It's not enough to just show and explain; you must also encourage students, colleagues and those whom you mentor or coach to follow their own interests and pursue knowledge on their own.

In school two, during a performance management review, and just before I applied for Future Leaders the first time, I asked my head of department (who was also my line manager) for help. I had put together my documents and needed her to give me some ideas for my next steps to work on. She surprised me with her response. In simple terms, she told me that she was the wrong person to ask. She felt that I was now beyond the point where she could be of service to me. She was a great leader, who knew that she could no longer give me guidance, and she directed me to start to look further outwards for development instead of limiting my growth. For clarity, it was her that put the Future Leaders flyer on my desk. It was a selfless act. She lost a great maths teacher – a simple decision that opened another path for me to walk down. By encouraging me to continue to develop, she propelled me on to my next step.

It's very much part of the British culture, particularly in London, to ask people what they do (for a job) when you first meet them. This is very different from Aussie culture and, as a direct consequence, I know many people from a range of backgrounds, as my initial interactions when meeting people have always been very different to those of my British counterparts. I like people; I like to learn about others and learn from them. I believe that it's the foundation of my 'why'. The author of *Start with Why* (2011), Simon Sinek, looks at that which inspires us and acts as the source of all that we do. My 'why' is to develop people and to create and build things. It is apparent that I have been around people or perhaps drawn to those who have developed me consciously or subconsciously all of my life. They have helped to build the me that I am today. There is no doubt that I have become the CEO of the Mossborne Federation and Progress Teaching because of my relentless hard work, but it is equalled by the combined efforts of everyone I've ever known who has helped me along the path to overcome the many setbacks that I have faced. Glen Denham told us about the importance of finding your leadership tribe, and I am so blessed that I found mine. My knockbacks taught me humility and gave me a reminder that there is always more to learn. My successes taught me the value of resilience and the importance of moving out of my comfort zone and into the unknown.

Leadership skills

Exploration: The action of exploring an unfamiliar area

Doing the unfamiliar is daunting. For you, the unfamiliar territory may be preparing for and starting the first year of being in post as a principal. In this section, I will guide you through the process of exploring an unfamiliar area by detailing my first year as principal. Every school needs work, even the outstanding ones. Therefore, you very quickly need a plan. Put it on a sticky note, Excel document or school development plan – it doesn't matter where – but you do need one. It doesn't have to be pretty but there is no grace period and time will work at super speed. I had a notebook.

There are lots of books written about what to do in the first 100 days, some of which I have since read. But I thought that it would be more helpful to share with you the reality of my first year (195 days) rather than talk about a piece of business theory. In my case, stepping into the big shoes of my predecessor and the role meant that all of the theory went out of the window. I was following on from the founder who started the organisation. He had an evangelical following – so much so that I liken him to the infamous Steve Jobs of Apple. People would just do what he wanted because he had credibility and commanded respect.

I was appointed and two vice-principals walked out the door. One of them actively recruited staff to his new school from mine, meaning that I had a constant stream of staff departures. By my first summer break, 30-plus teachers – almost a third of the teaching body – from all different levels (teachers to senior leaders) had left. To make matters worse, this mass exodus was clearly making some of my governors nervous about their new appointment. One governor even took it upon themselves to conduct a survey about me with staff behind my back. I'm thankful to say that when this was brought to the attention of the chair and deputy chair of the governing board, they saw it for what it was, met with me without judgement to discuss it and looked at a way forward. This was a tough moment, but there were many more.

Some people will leverage moments for their own benefit, and as a new principal you won't always see it when it is happening. They are the people who will ask for ridiculous salaries because they can, or attempt to influence their career by threatening you with their departure if they are not promoted into the role that they want. There are the people who will expect you to lower standards, as they believe that it's the way to hold onto the people who are left.

Some people want the school to be successful and will support you. They will rally around you in different ways. They are the people who offer advice that you may be too defensive to take at the time but will come to rely on once you realise that they are allies. These are the people who give you the true pulse of the school mood without it being idle gossip. They are the people who will correct the naysayers and put them in their place and you will never know it.

Some people will lay low and wait for the dust to settle. These are the people that are often hidden gems. They are the consistent ones who have often stayed away from the limelight and just focused on doing a good job for the school and for the children. These are the ones that don't see themselves as leaders but are the quiet supporters watching from afar.

In my first year I needed to focus on:

1. maintaining outcomes and standards

2. building a new school: Mossbourne Victoria Park

3. developing and planning the next steps for Mossbourne.

While some staff were leveraging the period of change, there were the others who wanted the school to continue to do well for the children and the community – the staff who came in every day, like they always had, and did a great job for their children and their team. There were people who I could trust to help me with tasks or projects that needed to be done and who would restabilise the school while the second Mossbourne was being built. I had no choice but to keep the plan simple:

- Walk the corridors; keep it tight.
- Focus on teaching and learning.
- Recruit, recruit, recruit.
- Talk to leaders, especially the middle leaders.

But it worked. Whatever noise confronts you, address it full on but also keep moving in the right direction. Sometimes communities face adversity that can come in many forms and can become all-consuming, but it can also help you to grow – grow as an individual and grow as a team. Resilience is your capacity to bounce back from adversity and learn from the challenge (or challenges) presented to you.

As the team developed, I was able to move on to the next step and the next step and the next step. We started to codify Mossbourne. We looked at teaching and learning tools that could help us and we built on the successes. Within a blink of an eye, two, three or four years pass by, and you look around seeing the fruits of your labour and the impact of the hard work and focus. I do not say this all as a deterrent but, no matter how many stories or '100 day' books you read, nothing prepares you for headship more than doing the job itself. Everything about the role is an exploration. When coming into any school there is a huge element of change management, riding the storm and finding the key players for your team. While the first year was difficult, it was a huge learning experience and I wouldn't change it.

Background: The circumstances or situation prevailing at a particular time or underlying a particular event

According to Simon Sinek (2011), it's 'The compelling higher purpose that inspires us and acts as the source of all we do.' At Mossbourne, we have three values that ensure that we are all on the same path:

- **excellence:** doing everything as well as we can – always
- **no excuses:** believing that anything is possible – we just have to know how
- **unity:** working together towards our goals – with integrity.

In this section, I explain the background and the beginning of the codification of Mossbourne, which started with our values (and the mission). It's important to know who you are, what you stand for, what you won't stand for and where you want to go. We get the 'where' from the mission, as it gives us the destination, and as leaders we set the path for others to follow. The values are the non-negotiables that are interwoven into the fabric of our schools.

I am often asked how we do what we do and what our blueprint is. I have given this information freely throughout this book, but the values and their meanings are unique. Although some words are used frequently across schools, it is the meaning behind them that is different, and that is what truly defines them for an organisation. People have different motivations and perceptions of belonging, but this is it for us.

Excellence

It is often connected with qualities such as dedication, hard work, perseverance, attention to detail and a passion for continuous improvement. It can therefore be demonstrated in many areas of life, such as academics, sports, the arts and personal relationships. Because it is a standard for which people strive, it requires a combination of talent, effort and determination to achieve. It is a hallmark of quality and success. In a world that doesn't always offer equity to our children, we ensure that they receive what they need in order to achieve their goals, however unique it may be to them.

No excuses

The key elements that make up a no-excuse mindset are establishing clear expectations about what needs to be accomplished and not being afraid to have a go. This is directed at the staff, stakeholders and children. Ensuring that students have the knowledge and skills to progress towards their aspirations is enabling and a highly effective motivator. Often in state education we talk about the problems that children have – why they can't do something. Excuses are popular – look at Hackney Downs School. But what I say is that state school pupils, especially those from poorer, challenging backgrounds such as mine, need to do more not less. If you are already behind, how does doing less help? Doing less is popular. Making excuses is popular, but we need to be honest and say that doing the same isn't enough – you need to do more. There are no limits. There are no excuses. Our staff do what is right for our children because we believe in equity.

Unity

It's coming together instead of being divided. It's Veronica, my vice-principal, showing our graduate teacher (who would go on to become the principal of the same school) that even when it's raining, we stand outside together on the school gate to welcome the children in, because that's what our students deserve and expect. It's what the graduate-teacher-turned-principal now does when he has new recruits. They join him on the gates to welcome his cohorts of children into school on rainy, windy or even snowy days. This may sound like a little thing to use as an example. But wisdom teaches you that the little things become the big things.

Our core values are **excellence**, **no excuses** and **unity**. They are the magic behind the mission and the partnership between all stakeholders.

Case study: Dr Timothy Wiens, Principal (pre-school to 12th grade), USA

Introduction

I met Tim, an inspirational leader, during my Executive MBA at Oxford University. Tim has a passion for learning that resulted in him travelling to the UK for an EMBA once a month for two years – a huge commitment not only to his own professional development but also to the development of the institution in which he works for his students. I've always admired Tim's integrity and purpose; he is someone who walks the walk and does what he says he is going to do. He is a dedicated Christian and academic, who has contributed to research and peer reviews. He is the head of a large independent school, with approximately 1,300 pupils, in Atlanta, Georgia, USA. Prior to this, he served in the public school system in the inner city of Chicago and has also worked in higher education as a lecturer.

Case study

Thirty-one years ago, I chose to pursue my life's vocation as an educator. To date, I have worked as a teacher, coach, dean of students, headmaster and university professor. I have worked in the US public and private school systems, within a boarding school in Switzerland and at several colleges and universities. Throughout each step of my journey, the weight of the responsibility to educate other people's children and prepare them to flourish as citizens and productive, winsome members of society has not been lost on me. The reality is that being an educator is far more than a career. As mentioned previously, education has been and will always be my vocation – my calling in life. It is far more than just a pay cheque. My life as an educator is a challenge to engage the children whom I am responsible for educating in a manner that enables them to better understand themselves and the role that they play in the world around them. Being an educator is about impacting hearts and minds and preparing students to do likewise, no matter the career that they may one day choose. Human flourishing is the goal.

In 2002, at the age of 32, I received my first call from an urban school in the heart of Boston, Massachusetts to lead as its headmaster. I had spent much of my career to that point as a full-time history teacher and soccer coach in mostly affluent schools, and was now responsible for leading a school where many came from low-income homes, arriving on our doorstep several grade levels behind. Now, I was responsible for guiding this institution, its faculty, its students and even its parents, as the school head.

In taking on this role, I think that I was naive and maybe even, unknowingly, had some hubris, in that I never thought twice about my lack of experience, the cultural differences or my privileged educational background. I believed that I could do the work and could lead the school towards excellence in a manner that was appropriate. I came quickly to realise that with this challenge came great responsibility. To speak to the title of this book chapter, I knew that I had big shoes to fill. However, I did not know what I did not know, and much learning was to take place in the days and years ahead.

When I first arrived on the scene, the chairman of my board of trustees made sure to introduce me to some local community and school leaders. While I did not fully comprehend it at the time, I know that my board chair did; these stalwarts would help to shape my future as a leader and as a man. The Reverend F. Washington (Tony) Jarvis, then headmaster at The Roxbury Latin School, the oldest school in the United States, became my first mentor. He took me under his wing, knowing that, as a young leader, I needed support and guidance. He knew what it meant to fill such big shoes. With me, he shared his insights as a 30-plus-years headmaster at one of the most prestigious schools in the world. He shared his time. He shared handbooks and policies and allowed me to utilise them as my own. He also shared his success stories and the stories of his failures – all lessons that I needed to hear and learn. All that he had, he offered to me.

As Tony was nearing retirement, in his wisdom my board chairman also introduced me to William (Bill) L. Burke III, the headmaster of St Sebastian's School. Bill, also a legend in the independent school world, picked up right where Tony left off when he retired. Bill filled the role of mentor and shared his wisdom with me over years. In fact, to this day, Bill still imparts his wisdom to me and shapes my thinking on what it means to be a school leader. Any time I call, he picks up the phone.

Both men have provided their support at no personal gain. Neither had an agenda other than to help a young school leader to grow and learn how to make an impact. Both recognised the need to invest in the heart and mind of a novice leader who sought to provide an education to young people, many of whom came from difficult homes, tough neighbourhoods and rough backgrounds. Both knew that their investment in me was an investment in the lives of the thousands of students that I would have the opportunity to empower over the course of my career. Today, I recognise that their selfless leadership – servant leadership, if you will – has helped to shape the person that I am, the leader that I am and the educator that I am. As I consider what it means to 'stand on the shoulders of giants' and to invest in the next generation of both students and school leaders, it is my hope and prayer that I may impact the hearts and minds of my students, faculty and any person whom I am blessed to mentor in such a manner, just as they have done for me.

The responsibility of being an educational leader, whether in the classroom or as a school administrator, is one that comes with great responsibility. Such responsibility is more than simply providing a great education that prepares students for university or the workforce. It is a responsibility that comes with an understanding that my role is to impact and shape young people, to help them to realise who they are, and to allow them to achieve more than they, or maybe even I, could have imagined or dreamed. Today, considering what it means to fill big shoes is to consider what it means to serve others before oneself, to listen intently, to give when you receive nothing in return and to seek to grow future generations who will do likewise. The educational leader who does these things will gain an eternal benefit that will continue long after the work is complete.

The solution

Be yourself

Don't try to take on your predecessor's personality or leadership style or be someone who you're not. Being unapologetically authentic will earn you respect and help to pre-empt judgement from others who are likely to compare you to your predecessor.

Team

You'll want to assess whether you have the right team with whom to accomplish your key priorities. This includes hiring to fill any gaps, as well as directly addressing performance issues that can prevent you from getting the leverage that you need or impede your progress.

Mindset

Having big shoes to fill can make you question your own capabilities and whether you have what it takes to meet the standard set by your predecessor. Imposter syndrome is not uncommon, especially as you become more senior and are faced with completely new challenges. Even if there is evidence to the contrary, you may feel like a fraud or question whether you can measure up to the standard set before you. This is normal to some extent, but it's something to manage as you get your bearings. Don't get into a negative spiral; you are in exactly the place in which you are meant to be.

Seek ongoing feedback and support

Create feedback loops with your key individuals for them to share early and often about what's going well and what's not, so that you can make real-time adjustments as and when needed. Recognise that giving upward feedback can feel daunting for your team and very risky, so you will need to give them your explicit permission to do so. Your job is to then listen – if you don't, it's likely that they will not try a second time, and you will not get the information that you need to hear.

The final words

Nothing can prepare you for the actual weight of being a principal. I was an acting co-principal before taking on the substantive post, and I thought that would have prepared me, but it didn't. The whole weight of the school, the staff, the children and their future descends on your shoulders like the mythological Greek Titan Atlas, who carried the world on his shoulders. Everyone has ideas about how things should be, but ultimately you have to make the decision.

A few days into my role, I had an epiphany at the school gate. It hit me that my name was on the door now, but there was also the stark reminder as I watched the children walk past me, ready to start their day, that the school of which I was now the leader was in the top one per cent of the country and needed to stay there or I would lose my job.

In an SLT meeting, when I was finally an official member of the team and before my headship had begun, we had all been arguing about something (professionally, of course). We were in a heated debate. There was disagreement with a decision that the principal had made. The discourse had the passion that you find in a high-functioning senior leadership team, boardroom or executive team environment. I can't even remember what the 'discussion' was about, but what I do remember is what my principal said to us all when he interrupted our debate: 'When it all goes wrong, or if it goes wrong, you will all have jobs, because it will be my neck on the line and not yours.' There is no greater truth as a leader.

In Act III, Scene I, of the William Shakespeare play *King Henry IV*, the title character says, 'Deny it to a king? Then happy low, lie down. Uneasy lies the head that wears a crown.' What Shakespeare is communicating here is how much responsibility kings carry – but I go to Stormzy's lyrics from the song 'Crown' on his 2019 *Heavy is the Head* album, because I am grateful for responsibility. Even if you disagree with someone's leadership style, it's a gift to be able to see great leaders in action on a day-to-day basis.

- **The buck stops with you:** If something is working well, it's you. If something isn't working well, it's you. Everyone has an opinion and a view. Listen to what they have to say but, in the end, you make the final decision because the accountability is yours. The school rises and falls based on what you do, and don't do, and you can't blame anyone else.

- **Don't be a sheep:** Don't let your head be turned with every passing trend, but also don't do the same thing that you've always done and expect a different outcome. Remember the first academies without walls that I spoke about? They thought that 'radical' meant that you had to change everything about teaching, even the building. But they forgot what our job and core business of a school is: teaching and learning. I always asked three questions in SLT: What's happening with the teaching? What's happening with the learning? What's happening with behaviour?

- **Keep It Simple Stupid (KISS):** Don't overcomplicate it; we don't ever need a million initiatives. You need the right people in the right jobs and great teachers in the classroom. The children are in school, receiving great lessons. This is the core business, but this shouldn't and doesn't take away from the tremendously important work of the support staff, who help to make this possible and take the noise away from teaching and learning so that the magic can happen.

When you have big shoes to fill, you will also likely feel that there are few people with whom you can confide about the tests that you face. This can be a challenge and sometimes isolating. I always bring my authentic self to work – for me, there is no other option – however, this doesn't mean that you are exactly the same person in every environment. I don't take my personal problems to work – my friends and family also have a unique part of me that is just for them.

You need people around you whom you can trust. I had my vice principal, Veronica Carol, to begin with, but the group of people grew and grew. Look for them – they are there and you will need them because it's lonely at the top. People will lie to you, people will try to discredit you, people will tell you their interpretation of the pulse of the organisation. You need to quickly identify those who are purposely looking for and collecting stories because they genuinely believe that's their job; those looking for problems for you to solve because they think it's the right thing to do; and those who actually know the lay of the land and have objectivity.

Top tips

- You will have setbacks; learn from them and go again.
- Listen to people, give them autonomy but remember that the buck stops with you.
- Find your champions; they are the people who will make your leadership possible.
- Never, ever lower your standards.

9 Where to from here?

By now, I think that you've probably come to realise that I am not one to shy away from the hard topics or conversations. Therefore, in this final chapter, I wanted to focus on the message that I'm hoping you have picked up on a few of the threads as you've travelled with me along the many paths of my life that have brought me to this present moment: education in England is a wicked problem.

A wicked problem is one that is difficult or virtually impossible to solve. This is normally because there are contradictory or even changing requirements. Sounds familiar? Education is a social (and cultural) wicked problem. It is difficult to solve because, although we can all agree that we want children to go to 'good' schools and receive a great education, we can't agree on what defines a 'good' school or exactly what a great education should include. For that matter, in England, we can't even decide what type of school (academy, local authority, voluntary added) is best. So, instead of focusing on the fact that I work within the storm of a wicked problem – something that is known to be unsolvable – I'm going to focus on what I feel is important to us – to the trust in which I work – and elaborate on the 'why'.

I have never seen myself as the owner of Mossbourne. I am its custodian. I'm here to nurture it, to help it to grow and to leave it in a better place than where I found it. The goal – the journey – is not focused on today and not focused on tomorrow but on 100 years from now. I did not take this job for the short-term gains; this was about creating a school and, ultimately, a legacy that would be around in 100 years. Although modern science is great, in 100 years I will be dead. Yet when I reflect on institutions that have lasted, they are long-lasting because their success has become self-perpetuating. The journey never ends. To become self-perpetuating, Mossbourne needs to be run by Mossbournians, and ultimately, one will one day be its CEO. A school or even a trust being run by a member of its community can play a significant role in enabling it to take charge of its education, its future and its children's future.

Every second school in England has the word 'community' in its title, but what does it mean to be a community school? Surely the ultimate aim of a community school is for it to be run by (yes, you've guessed it) its community. However, please don't mistake my words; schools should not be run by committees or be at the whim of the latest trend. I'd like to reimagine the term 'community school', because sometimes things need to be reimagined for the modern world.

A school should serve its community, right? At Mossbourne, we mapped out the journey to this goal. The journey to creating a community for a school and trust has clear 'mile' markers:

- **Mile marker 1:** Create a school to which you would send your children.
- **Mile marker 2:** Staff seek to send their own children there.
- **Mile marker 3:** Alumni become teachers.
- **Mile marker 4:** Alumni send their children to the school.
- **Mile marker 5:** Alumni become governors.
- **Mile marker 6:** Alumni become principal.
- **Mile marker 7:** Alumni become CEO and chair of governors.

Mossbourne passed mile marker 5 this year. It was a proud moment to have a former student – a practising doctor – as a governor. We are well on our way to creating a true community federation. This isn't about not letting outsiders in, of course, but about creating traditions and legacies that can evolve and enable the next leaders to continue the journey. I came into the community knowing the level of expectation, traditional values and responsibility that I needed and wanted to bring into the role. I feel privileged to have been allowed to lead this part of Mossbourne's journey.

For me, leadership is a privilege. A gift. An honour. There is no greater honour than serving your community by leading one of its schools.

Further reading

Aha! (n.d.), 'Themes, epics, stories, and tasks', www.aha.io/roadmapping/guide/agile/themes-vs-epics-vs-stories-vs-tasks

Ambition Institute (n.d.), 'Programmes', www.ambition.org.uk/programmes

Babineaux, R. and Krumboltz, J. (2014), *Fail Fast, Fail Often: How losing can help you win*. New York: Tarcher.

Bennett, N. (2018), 'Fail fast, fail often – why failure will make you successful', LinkedIn Pulse, www.linkedin.com/pulse/fail-fast-often-why-failure-make-you-successful-nick-bennett

Cardona, P. and Rey, C. (2022), 'Missions-driven leadership', in *Management by Missions*. Cham: Springer, pp. 131–45.

Corkindale, G. (2008), 'Overcoming imposter syndrome', *Harvard Business Review*, 7 May 2008, https://hbr.org/2008/05/overcoming-imposter-syndrome

Department for Education (DfE) (2017), 'Widening participation in higher education, England, 2014/15 age cohort', https://assets.publishing.service.gov.uk/government/uploads/system/uploads/attachment_data/file/635103/SFR39-2017-MainText.pdf

Department for Education (DfE) (2019), 'National statistics: school and college performance tables in England: 2017 to 2018', www.fenews.co.uk/skills/national statistics-school-and-college-performance-tables-in-england-2017-to-2018

Education Endowment Foundation (EEF) (2022), 'Using your pupil premium funding effectively', https://educationendowmentfoundation.org.uk/guidance-for-teachers/using-pupil-premium

Envoplan (2019), 'The challenge of designing a school for the 21st century', https://envoplan.co.uk/education-news/the-challenge-of-designing-a-school-for-the-21st-century

Guardian (2011), 'Letters: Closing the achievement gap in our schools', 18 August 2011, www.theguardian.com/education/2011/aug/18/closing-achievement-gap-in-schools

Kniberg, H. (2019), 'Spotify engineering culture – part 1 (aka the "Spotify Model")', YouTube, www.youtube.com/watch?v=Yvfz4HGtoPc

London Youth Rowing (n.d.), 'Mossbourne Rowing Academy', www.londonyouthrowing.com/programmes/mossbourne-rowing-academy

Millard, W., Bowen-Viner, K., Baars, S., Trethewey, A. and Menzies, L. (2018), 'Boys on track: improving support for Black Caribbean and free school meal-eligible White boys in London', LKMco, www.london.gov.uk/sites/default/files/lkmco_boys_on_track_report.pdf

Ministry of Housing, Communities and Local Government (2019), 'The English Indicators of Deprivation 2019', https://assets.publishing.service.gov.uk/government/uploads/system/uploads/attachment_data/file/835115/IoD2019_Statistical_Release.pdf

Moore, R. L. and Gillette, D. (2001), *King, Warrior, Magician, Lover: Rediscovering the archetypes of the mature masculine*. San Francisco: Harper San Francisco.

Mustafa, R. (2012), 'With stars in their A's, Mossbourne students aim for university courses', East London Lines, www.eastlondonlines.co.uk/2012/08/with-stars-in-their-as-mossbourne-students-align-dreams-to-university-courses

Ofsted (2015), 'A level subject take-up', www.gov.uk/government/publications/a-level-subject-take-up

Porter, S. H. (2018), 'You win or you learn: risk-taking for leaders', Forbes, www.forbes.com/sites/forbescoachescouncil/2018/01/11/you-win-or-you-learn-risk-taking-for-leaders/?sh=6f3ffc793e5c

Progress Teaching (n.d.), 'Understanding where your school is on its improvement journey', https://progressteaching.com/understanding-where-your-school-is-on-its-improvement-journey

Russell Group (2017), 'Subject choices at school and college', http://russellgroup.ac.uk/for-students/school-and-college-in-the-uk/subject-choices-at- school-and-college

Saifi, N. (2022), 'What is an epic? (Definition, meaning and examples)', Chisel glossary, https://chisellabs.com/blog/what-is-epic-in-agile

Social Mobility Commission (2017), 'Time for change: an assessment of government policies on social mobility 1997–2017', https://assets.publishing.service.gov.uk/government/uploads/system/uploads/attachment_data/file/622214/Time_for_Change_report_-_An_assessement_of_government_policies_on_social_mobility_1997-2017.pdf

Sutton Trust (2015), 'Developing teachers: improving professional development for teachers', www.suttontrust.com/wp-content/uploads/2019/12/Developing-Teachers-1.pdf

Trust for London (2020), 'London's poverty profile: Boroughs: Hackney', https://trustforlondon.org.uk/data/boroughs/hackney-poverty-and-inequality-indicators/?indicator=people

van Kleef, G. A., Heerdink, M. W., Cheshin, A., Stamkou, E., Wanders, F., Koning, L. F., Fang, X. and Georgeac, O. A. M. (2021), 'No guts, no glory? How risk-taking shapes dominance, prestige, and leadership endorsement', *Journal of Applied Psychology*, 106, (11), 1673–94.

Walsh, D. (2021), 'Are leaders rewarded for taking risks?', Yale Insights, https://insights.som.yale.edu/insights/are-leaders-rewarded-for-taking-risks

Wrike (2021), 'What is agile methodology in project management?', www.wrike.com/project-management-guide/faq/what-is-agile-methodology-in-project-management

References

BBC Radio 4 (2016), 'How to turn your life around', www.bbc.co.uk/programmes/b074xbs4

Beck, K., Beedle, M., van Bennekum, A. et al. (2001), 'The Agile Manifesto', Agile Alliance, http://agilemanifesto.org

Bolton, P. (2021), 'Oxbridge "elitism"', House of Commons Library, https://researchbriefings.files.parliament.uk/documents/SN00616/SN00616.pdf

Busby, E. (2019), 'Oxford University to offer free year of study to disadvantaged students with lower grades', *Independent*, 21 May 2019, www.independent.co.uk/news/education/education-news/oxford-university-poorer-students-admission-diversity-social-mobility-a8922366.html

Clear, J. (n.d.), 'This coach improved every tiny thing by 1 percent and here's what happened', James Clear, https://jamesclear.com/marginal-gains

Coe, R., Aloisi, C., Higgins, S. and Major, L. E. (2014), 'What makes great teaching? Review of the underpinning research', Sutton Trust, www.suttontrust.com/wp-content/uploads/2019/12/What-makes-great-teaching-FINAL-4.11.14-1.pdf

Collins, J. and Hansen, M. T. (2011), *Great by Choice: Uncertainty, chaos, and luck – why some thrive despite them all*. New York: Harper Business.

Collis, D. and Rukstad, M. (2008), 'Strategy and competition: can you say what your strategy is?', *Harvard Business Review*, April 2008, https://hbr.org/2008/04/can-you-say-what-your-strategy-is

Conklin, J. and Weil, W. (2007), 'Wicked problems: naming the pain in organizations', Touchstone, www.accelinnova.com/docs/wickedproblems.pdf

Covey, S. R. (1989), *The Seven Habits of Highly Effective People: Restoring the character ethic*. New York: Simon and Schuster.

Crime Rate UK (2023), 'Crime and safety in Hackney', https://crimerate.co.uk/london/hackney

Education Endowment Foundation (EEF) (2022), 'The EEF guide to the pupil premium', https://d2tic4wvo1iusb.cloudfront.net/documents/guidance-for-teachers/pupil-premium/Pupil_Premium_Guide_Apr_2022_1.0.pdf

Francis, B., Taylor, B. and Tereshchenko, A. (2019), *Reassessing 'Ability' Grouping: Improving practice for equity and attainment*. London: Routledge.

Frery, F., Lecocq, X. and Warnier, V. (2015), 'Competing with ordinary resources', *MIT Sloan Management Review*, 56, (3), 69.

Gardner, H. and Laskin, E. (2011), *Leading Minds: An anatomy of leadership*. New York: Basic Books.

Goffee, R. and Jones, G. (1996), 'What holds the modern company together?', *Harvard Business Review*, 74, (6), 133 –48.

Greater London Authority (2017), 'Population Hackney', www.hackney.gov.uk/population

Green, E. (2010), *Building a better teacher, The New York Times*. Available at: https://www.nytimes.com/2010/03/07/magazine/07Teachers-t.html (Accessed: 17 May 2023).

Hackney Learning Trust (2017a), 'Post 16 forecasts SCAP 2017', London Borough of Hackney.

Hackney Learning Trust (2017b), 'Hackney's secondary schools: 2017 admission guide for parents', London Borough of Hackney, https://issuu.com/hackneylearningtrust/docs/hlt16_secondary_issuu

Hayes, A. (2022), 'Vertical integration explained: how it works, with types and examples', Investopedia, www.investopedia.com/terms/v/verticalintegration.asp

Jestico + Whiles (2023), 'Projects: Mossbourne Victoria Park Academy', www.jesticowhiles.com/projects/mossbourne-victoria-park-academy

Kahneman, D. (2011), *Thinking, Fast and Slow*. New York: Farrar, Straus and Giroux.

Kim, C. and Mauborgne, R. (1997), 'Value innovation: the strategic logic of high growth', *Harvard Business Review*, 75, (1), 102 –12.

Lean Manufacturing Tools (2017), 'Seven wastes of service | Customer perception', http://leanmanufacturingtools.org/81/seven-wastes-of-service-customer-perceptio

Lemov, D. (2010), *Teach Like a Champion*. Hoboken, NJ: Jossey-Bass.

Meehan, R. J. (n.d.), Homepage, http://robertjohnmeehan.com

Mintzberg, H. (1998), 'Covert leadership: notes on managing professionals', *Harvard Business Review*, 76, (6), 140 –7.

ModelThinkers (2022), 'Stockdale paradox', https://modelthinkers.com/mental-model/stockdale-paradox

Montacute, R. and Cullinane, C. (2018), 'Access to Advantage: The influence of schools and place on admissions to top universities' rep. Sutton Trust. Available at: https://www.suttontrust.com/wp-content/uploads/2018/12/Access-to-Advantage.pdf.

Office for Fair Access (2018), 'Annual report and accounts 2017 –18', https://assets.publishing.service.gov.uk/government/uploads/system/uploads/attachment_data/file/728202/2017-18_OFFA_annual_report_2307FINAL.PDF

Office for National Statistics (ONS) (2022), 'Key stage 4 performance 2019 (revised)', Department for Education, www.gov.uk/government/statistics/key-stage-4-performance-2019-revised

Office for Students (2023), 'Consultation on a new approach to regulating equality of opportunity: analysis of responses and decisions', www.officeforstudents.org.

uk/publications/consultation-on-a-new-approach-to-regulating-equality-of-opportunity-analysis-of-responses/commentary

Ofsted (2021), 'Inspection of Mossbourne Community Academy', https://files.ofsted.gov.uk/v1/file/50171741

Oxford College of Marketing (n.d.), 'What is a PESTEL analysis', https://blog.oxfordcollegeofmarketing.com/2016/06/30/pestel-analysis

Pascale, R., Milleman, M. and Gioja, L. (1997), 'Changing the way we change: how leaders at Sears, Shell, and the U.S. Army transformed attitudes and behavior – and made the changes stick', *Harvard Business Review*, 75, (6), 126–39.

Pierson, R. (n.d.), 'Every kid needs a champion', TED Talk, www.ted.com/talks/rita_pierson_every_kid_needs_a_champion

Powell, T. (2006), 'Unlock the deep structure of competitive performance', *Strategy Magazine*, 9, 9–14.

Rustin, S. (2007), 'The Saturday interview: Mossbourne Academy's Sir Michael Wilshaw', *Guardian*, 17 September 2011, www.theguardian.com/theguardian/2011/sep/17/michael-wilshaw-interview

Select Committee on Education and Skills (2003), 'Memorandum submitted by White Hart Lane School', https://publications.parliament.uk/pa/cm200203/cmselect/cmeduski/513/3040711.htm

Sheppard, J. M. and Young, W. B. (2006), 'Agility literature review: classifications, training and testing', *Journal of Sports Sciences*, 24, 919–32.

Sinek, S. (2011), *Start with Why: How great leaders inspire everyone to take action*. London: Penguin Books.

Stebbings, J. and Dopson, S. (2018), 'Inspirational Leadership Inspired By Shakespeare's Henry V', Olivier Mythodrama, London.

Stone, J. (2021), 'Local indicators of child poverty after housing costs, 2020/21', Loughborough University, https://repository.lboro.ac.uk/articles/report/Local_indicators_of_child_poverty_after_housing_costs_2020_21/20974252

Sutton Trust (2008), 'University admissions by individual schools', www.suttontrust.com/wp-content/uploads/2019/12/UniversityAdmissions-1.pdf

Sutton Trust (2011a), 'Improving the impact of teachers on pupil achievement in the UK – interim findings', www.suttontrust.com/wp-content/uploads/2019/12/2teachers-impact-report-final-1.pdf

Sutton Trust (2011b), 'Degrees of success: university chances by individual school', www.suttontrust.com/wp-content/uploads/2019/12/sutton-trust-he-destination-report-final-1.pdf

Sutton Trust (2016), 'Teachers' Oxbridge perceptions polling', www.suttontrust.com/research-paper/teachers-oxbridge-perceptions-polling

Sutton Trust (2021), 'Universities and social mobility: summary report', www.suttontr ust.com/wp-content/uploads/2021/11/Universities-and-social-mobility-final- summary.pdf

Teach Like a Champion (n.d.), Homepage, https://teachlikeachampion.org

The Children's Society (n.d.), 'What is county lines?', www.childrenssociety.org.uk/ what-we-do/our-work/child-criminal-exploitation-and-county-lines/what-is- county-lines

UCAS Analysis & Research (2017), UCAS End of Cycle report 2017: Executive Summary. rep. UCAS. Available at: https://www.ucas.com/sites/default/files/exec_summa ry_wave4_finalcover.pdf.

Wiliam, D. (2017), *Embedded formative assessment*. Bloomington, IN: Solution Tree Press.

Woodhouse, A. (2016), 'Viewpoint: how we learn to believe in ourselves', BBC News, 22 March 2016, www.bbc.co.uk/news/magazine-35911187

Woolcock, N. (2022), 'No excuses: the mantra and rowing boat that will help academy take on Eton', *The Times*, 26 March 2022, www.thetimes.co.uk/article/no-excu ses-the-mantra-and-rowing-boat-that-will-help-academy-take-on-eton- thc7c7f65

Wykeham, O. and Madison, M. (2020), 'Bowen space hub "awesome" news for aspiring rocket scientist, regional officials', *ABC News*, 28 July 2020, www.abc.net. au/news/2020-07-29/bowen-rocket-site-exciting-news-for-young-aviation-ent husiast/12500802

Index

ABCDE model 96–7
academisation programme 103–4
accountability 12, 13, 157
active learning 108, 109
adaptability 5–6
African and Caribbean pupils,
    underachievement of 9
agile framework 25–6
    embracing 26–7
    people support 28
    philosophy 26
    user-centric approach 28–9
Agile Manifesto 24–5
anti-racism 8, 9
archetypal leadership 87–8
architecture 54
arts, The 54
audits
    external 14
    financial 13–14
    internal 14
autistic child support 42

Beck, K. 24, 25
belief level of pupil 59–60
built environment 54

Carol, V. 141–2, 152, 157
case studies
    Bedborough, K. 72–4
    Cox, S. 94–7
    Denham, G. 134–7
    Hall, S. 55–9
    Ojja, M. 113–17
    Rutherford, N. 34–7
    Wiens, T. 152–5
change, responding to 24–5
Chief Inspector 12–13
communal culture 128, 131–2

community school 159–60
conflict, and cultural change 132, 133–4
Conklin, J. 23
continuous professional development
    (CPD) 75, 83, 96, 105, 106, 117
conversations, challenging 9
creativity, focus on 47–9
'Crown' (song) 156
cultural change 132–3
    and conflict 132, 133–4
    and identity 132, 133
    and learning 133, 134
    and power 132, 133
customer collaboration 24–5
cycling team, British 66–7

data, importance of 117
disadvantaged backgrounds, pupils
    from 107–8
dyslexic children 3, 4

educational research 108–9
Elephant Group, The 112–13
engagement with pupils 10
excellence 150, 151
exceptional schools, leadership
    in 19–20
external audits 14
external validation 78
extra-curricular activities 47

feedback
    seeking 155–6
    to teachers 68–70
Ferguson, Sir A. 20
financial audits 13–15
formal observations 66
fragmented culture 128
Frery, F. 49

Future Leaders programme 18, 42, 113, 134, 145–7

GCSE resits and vocational courses, elimination of 50
Gioja, L. 132–3
Gist, S. 43
Goffee, R. 127–8
grading lessons 66, 110
Great by Choice (Collins and Hansen) 70

Hackney 7–9
How to Turn Your Life Around (BBC show) 53

identity, and cultural change 132, 133
individuals and interactions 24–5
infrastructure 23–4
inspections 12
    financial audits 13–14
    regimes 12
    use of recommendations 14
institutional racism 9
internal audits 14

Jobs, S. 148
Jones, G. 127–8
Jones, M. 112
Jung, C. G. 87

Kahneman, D. 117
Keep It Simple Stupid (KISS) approach 157
key performance indicators (KPIs) 30
Kim, C. 49, 50
KIPP model 42

leaders
    character and qualities 87–8
    as coverts 87
    risk-taking characteristic of 74
leadership mission 21
leadership skills 107–13
    agility 24–6
    analysis 44–52
    data, significance of 52–5
    exploring unfamiliar area 22–4

and relationships 127–32
scrutiny 30–4
and talent 84–6
lead inspector 13
learning, and cultural change 133, 134
Lemov, D. 42, 66
little-and-often approach 83
looked-after child (LAC) 1

Mauborgne, R. 49, 50
mercenary culture 128, 131
meritocratic society 111–12
Milleman, M. 132–3
mindsets 116, 155
Mintzberg, H. 87
mission-driven leaders 17, 37–8
Moore, S. 43
Moyes, D. 20
Mythodrama, O. 87

networked culture 128, 130–1
no excuses 150, 151
non-negotiables 114–15

Odunsi, D. 1, 9–10
Ofsted 12
    validation 22
    framework and handbook 13
    reports, unappealable 13
outcomes 9, 47

Pascale, R. 132–3
passive supervision 142
pastoral system 100–2
PESTEL (political, economic, social, technological, environmental and legal) analysis 47
Phoenix Programme 82
Pierson, R. 122–3, 127
playground space 32
poverty, impact of 9, 52–3
Powell, T. 47
power, and cultural change 132, 133
practice, significance of 118
primary schools 77–9

ProgressTeaching 70, 83, 105

quality of the teaching 103–18

Reassessing 'Ability' Grouping (Francis) 108
recruitment process 84, 97–9
relationships 121–7, 138–40
   research 132–4
   and school culture 127–32
   solution 137–8
resignations, dealing with 98, 104–5
resilience 5, 150
responsibility, of being an educational
     leader 154
risks
   matrix 73–4
   consequence of avoiding 74
   key risks, and their mitigation 69
   and solution 74–6
   with staff 9
Rowing Academy, The 54
Rukstad, M. 47

school-based sixth forms, challenges
     in 44–7
school building 31–4
science, technology, engineering and
     mathematics (STEM) education 43
security and stability, feeling of 6, 41, 42
senior leader, becoming and being 143–8
   being yourself 155
   and excellence 150, 151
   feedback and support seeking 155–6
   and mindset 155
   and no excuses 150, 151
   and team 155
   unfamiliar area, exploration of 22–
     4, 148–50
   and unity 150, 152
Shakespeare, W. 156
Sheppard, J. M. 24
Sinek, S. 148, 150
60 per cent rule 72, 144
sociability 128–32
software, working 24–5

solidarity 128–32
specialist programme creation 50–2
staff mindset 116
staff retention 86, 98–9, 104–5
Start with Why (Sinek) 148
Stockdale Paradox 22
strategic decision-making 38, 47
strategic prospects 47
subject offer 47
support seeking 155–6
sustainable competitive advantage 47
Sutton Trust 107
   in practice 108–11
   reports 107–12
   teacher impacts 107

talents 81–2, 97–9
   archetypal leadership 87–94
   and leadership skills 84–6
   overt and covert leadership 94
teacher shortages, management of 49
Teach Like a Champion framework 42, 66
Team Sky 66, 67
team work 33, 37
Thinking, Fast and Slow (Kahneman) 117
3 Rs model 97

Umbrellagate 70–1
Uncommon Schools Network 42
unfamiliar area, exploration of 22–4, 148–50
unity 150, 152
up-or-out approach 117
user-centric approach 28–9
user stories 27

vertical integration 46, 49–50
victim, child as 70–1
vision turning into actions,
     significance of 115

Walker, R. 139
Weil, W. 23
wicked problem, education as 23, 26, 159
Wiliam, D. 108–9
Wilshaw, Sir M. 18, 20, 43

Author Biography

Reprinted with kind permission from Lucienne Jacobs

Peter J Hughes is a visionary leader and CEO of a prominent Multi-Academy Trust and of an innovative Ed Tech company, with an unwavering passion for education. He champions the transformative power of learning and its impact on shaping future generations.

Raised in a diverse and challenging environment, Peter cultivated a unique viewpoint framing his education approach. He began the first chapters of his life in his homeland of Australia, leaving with a Bachelor of Education and experience of teaching in New South Wales. Hughes's transformational move to the UK resulted in him developing one of the most successful MATs in England and completing an Executive MBA at Oxford University.

Drawing upon his personal experiences, he understands the importance of creating inclusive and empowering learning environments for young people. A core element of his work is dedicated to developing exceptional leaders and fostering the growth of great schools.

Peter continues to drive positive change through his professional writing, public speaking and commitment to the communities he works in.